O ALMIGHTY GOD, who hast knit together thine elect in one communion and fellowship, in the mystical body of thy Son Christ our Lord: Grant us grace so as to follow thy blessed Saints in all virtuous and godly living, that we may come to those unspeakable joys, which thou hast prepared for them that unfeignedly love thee; through Jesus Christ our Lord.

Book of Common Prayer

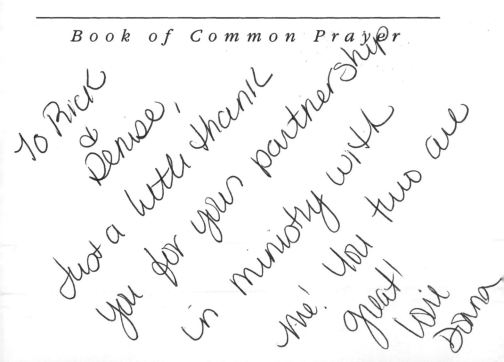

To Rick & Denise,
Just a little thank you for your partnership in ministry with me. You two are great!
Love,
Dana

Companions
for Your
SPIRITUAL
JOURNEY

Discovering
the Disciplines
of the Saints

MARK HARRIS

InterVarsity Press
Downers Grove, Illinois

InterVarsity Press
P.O. Box 1400, Downers Grove, IL 60515
World Wide Web: www.ivpress.com
E-mail: mail@ivpress.com

©1999 by Mark Harris

InterVarsity Press® is the book-publishing division of InterVarsity Christian Fellowship/USA®, a student movement active on campus at hundreds of universities, colleges and schools of nursing in the United States of America, and a member movement of the International Fellowship of Evangelical Students. For information about local and regional activities, write Public Relations Dept., InterVarsity Christian Fellowship/USA, 6400 Schroeder Rd., P.O. Box 7895, Madison, WI 53707-7895.

Scripture quotations, unless otherwise indicated, are from the New Revised Standard Version of the Bible, *copyright 1989 by the Division of Christian Education of the National Council of the Churches of Christ in the USA. Used by permission. All rights reserved.*

Poetry on page 38 taken from "For the Time Being," from W. H. Auden: Collected Poems *by W. H. Auden, edited by Edward Mendelson. Copyright © 1944 and renewed 1972 by W. H. Auden. Reprinted by permission of Random House, Inc.*

The Celtic Mass for the Sea *is quoted by permission of its composer, Scott Macmillan, and its librettist, Jennyfer Brickenden.*

Cover photograph: Bruce Hands/Tony Stone Images

ISBN 0-8308-2214-3

Printed in the United States of America ♾

Library of Congress Cataloging-in-Publication Data

Harris, Mark, 1958-
  Companions for your spiritual journey : discovering the
  disciplines of the saints / Mark Harris.
      p.   cm.
  Includes bibliographical references (p.).
  ISBN 0-8308-2214-3 (pbk. : alk. paper)
  1. Spiritual life—Christianity.   I. Title.
BV4501.2.H3598   1999
248.4—dc21

99-22819
CIP

| 17 | 16 | 15 | 14 | 13 | 12 | 11 | 10 | 9 | 8 | 7 | 6 | 5 | 4 | 3 | 2 |
| 12 | 11 | 10 | 09 | 08 | 07 | 06 | 05 | 04 | 03 | 02 | 01 | 00 | 99 |

FOR ADRIENNE
WHO HAS TAUGHT ME
THROUGH HER VERY LIVING
THAT "LOVE IS THE
ABRIDGEMENT OF ALL THEOLOGY."

FRANCIS DE SALES

ACKNOWLEDGMENTS 9

INTRODUCTION 11

THE INNER JOURNEY

ONE   JOURNEYING ON THE ROAD: *John Bunyan*. 17

TWO   TURNING OUR EYES ON JESUS: *Julian of Norwich* . . . 25

THREE PRACTICING THE PRESENCE OF JESUS:
           John of Ruysbroeck 34

FOUR   REACHING THE HIGHEST LOVE:
           Bernard of Clairvaux 42

OBSTACLES ON THE JOURNEY

FIVE   WORKING THROUGH SPIRITUAL DRYNESS:
           John Newton 53

SIX   COMBATING PRAYERLESSNESS: *Origen* 60

SEVEN RESISTING TEMPTATION: *The Desert Fathers* 67

EIGHT OVERCOMING DISCOURAGEMENT: *Evelyn Underhill*. . 75

THE OUTER JOURNEY

NINE   CELEBRATING SPIRITUAL FRIENDSHIPS:
           Aelred of Rievaulx. 87

TEN   LOVING THE UNLOVABLE: *Margery Kempe* 96

ELEVEN INSPIRING OTHERS TO GODLINESS: *George Herbert* . . 104

TWELVE CARING FOR CREATION: *The Celtic Saints*. 115

APPENDIX: *Reading the Saints* 124

NOTES 128

Acknowledgments

Blaise Pascal was not impressed with authors who incessantly referred to their work as "*my* book." Such an expression revealed not only their inflated egos but also their ignorance of how individual efforts invariably grow out of some kind of nurturing community. I want to thank the people who make up my nurturing community. In a profound sense this is *our* book.

I am grateful to two church communities full of friends in the faith: Grace Chapel in Halifax, Nova Scotia, and Wolfville United Baptist Church.

For the past sixteen years Inter-Varsity Christian Fellowship of Canada has been another formative Christian community in my life. In particular I want to thank four people—Tom Balke, Jim Berney, Barb Boyt and Barrett Horne. Technically they have been my bosses. Truth is, they have served me far more than I have served them. I will always be grateful for the freedom and trust they have extended to me in my spiritual pilgrimage.

Thanks too to friends who took time to read various chapters of this book and offer insightful advice: Tom and Kim Balke, my brother David Harris, David and Diane Langille, Pete Lawton and his small group, Derek Melanson, Heather Pyrcz, Andrew Steeves, Das Sydney and Trevor Tucker. I also want to thank friends at Gaspereau Press who graciously encouraged me to use revised portions of material from my previous book, *Three Faces of Jesus* (Gaspereau Press, 1997). I am grateful to Eric and Barb Ross and Peter Mackay and Heather Price for offering their cottages as quiet places to write, and to Debby Seary, who worked well beyond the call of duty in helping me prepare this manuscript.

From the beginning of this project I have received discerning advice and timely encouragement from InterVarsity Press. Thank you, Cindy Bunch-Hotaling.

In a book that celebrates the communion of saints, I would certainly be amiss if I failed to thank five present-day saints who have deeply shaped my spiritual life: my godly parents, Ron and Lorna Harris; my teacher and mentor, Harry Thompson; my soul friend, David Langille; and my exemplar and spiritual guide, Dr. James Houston. This book would never have been written without their love and inspiration.

Finally, I want to give special thanks to my family. To Emily, Laura and Dylan, who teach me so much and bring me so much joy, thanks for never begrudging Dad's time working on the book, even letting me slip downstairs to write every morning during our summer vacation on Prince Edward Island. To Adrienne, my wife, I owe gratitude beyond words.

Introduction

The seeds of this book were sown nine years ago when I spent a year studying at Regent College in Vancouver, British Columbia. One of the finest gifts of that year was being introduced to a rich tradition of devotional writing by saints who through the centuries have written with probing insight about what it means to have one's life transformed by the Holy Spirit.

Since that year I have endeavored to apprentice with some of these masters of the spiritual life. This book grows directly out of the confluence of my reading and living. For that reason, while the focus of this book is the wisdom of saints from the past, I am not averse to telling you some of my own stories from the present. I have learned a great deal from these masters; I want to introduce them to you not only as historical figures but as living companions who can shed light on the way of contemporary followers of Jesus.

Encountering these masters is not always easy. They are not even remotely interested in pandering to the public appetite for a warm and fuzzy spirituality. These are women and men who lived in the real world. They write from the head and the heart. They write from the depths, not the shallows. Still, every attempt to enter the sphere of their influence is more than worth the effort.

Through encountering their writings I have entered a world of strange new voices from cultures and historical settings far removed from my own. But instead of finding them unapproachable or irrelevant, I have discovered that these voices, shorn of contemporary cliché, have spoken directly and freshly to my heart. In fact, insofar as they are out of step with contemporary trends and obsessions, they are uniquely free to speak with bracing clarity to my own spiritual experience.

Living on the edge of the new millennium, it may seem that choosing to explore an age-old tradition of devotional writing is at best an exercise in nostalgia, at worst a spineless retreat from the dizzying challenges of the postmodern world, a harmless but ultimately pointless form of Christian antiquarianism. I don't believe that for a moment.

George Grant, the Canadian philosopher, was a fearless, penetrating critic of modernity. Near the end of his life Grant offered that he wanted to spend less time critiquing what was present in modernity, and more time reflecting about what was missing in modernity. As I have allowed the voices of the saints to speak to and inform my living, I have thought of this as my own small contribution to what must be an urgent task in our postmodern age—to rediscover what has been missing. The saints invite us to the experience of a vital, God-centered spirituality. They call us to be attentive to the intuitive and psychological dimensions of faith, the integration of mind and heart, and to schooling in the disciplines of genuine community and witness. As we enter a new millenium, we desperately need to hear their voices.

The voices I have chosen to explore in this book come from the three main branches of Christianity—Eastern Orthodox, Roman Catholic, and Protestant. Within each are vibrant traditions of Christian spirituality. While there are differences in perspective that emerge from these traditions, in the end it is the similarities that have left the deepest impression on me. All of these saints write about what it means to follow Jesus. Their lives have been transformed by him; his presence permeates their writing. Reading perspectives from outside our own tradition may call for discernment, but because Jesus is at the center of this canon of devotional writing, it does not call for defensiveness.

Together the saints form a "glorious company" (the phrase is taken from the ancient Christian prayer, the *Te Deum*). Walking the road of Christian pilgrimage with this glorious company makes me aware that I am a member of a community that transcends time—the communion of saints. Only the thinnest of veils separates the members, living or dead, of the mystical body of Christ.

But these men and women are glorious company in another sense. As I have sat under their instruction, they have become mentors and companions from whom I have drawn great strength and encouragement. They are indeed glorious company with whom to travel, wise and thoughtful friends whose witness can console and stir and inspire us, as together we walk the way of Jesus. My hope in writing this book is that I would adequately commend these companions and their wisdom to you, and that you would welcome their companionship on your own spiritual journey. They have become wonderful friends to me, and I wish and pray the same for you.

THE INNER JOURNEY

Being a Christian means setting out on an inner journey—a journey of following Jesus. Along the way we learn to obey him and imitate him. Above all we become his intimate friends, and our lives are transformed by that friendship. Jesus calls us to turn to him in all of life's experiences, to develop spiritual eyes acutely attuned to the signs of his presence. Gradually, we realize that Jesus has nothing less in view than a radically new creation of our very selves. John Bunyan, Julian of Norwich, John of Ruysbroeck and Bernard of Clairvaux are companions along the way. They invite us to join them on this inner journey of transformation, a journey of ever-deepening identification with Jesus.

ONE

JOURNEYING ON THE ROAD
John Bunyan

Lead me in the path of your commandments,
* for I delight in it.*
Turn my heart to your decrees,
* and not to selfish gain.*
Turn my eyes from looking at vanities;
* give me life in your ways.*

PSALM 119:35-37

A true Christian is known by a Christian life and not by the name Christian.
. . . A Christian must daily renew himself. . . . Daily he is to groan that he
might not be a false Christian.

JOHAAN ARNDT (1555-1621)

For the high road and the shortest road [to heaven]
is measured by desire and not by yards.

THE CLOUD OF UNKNOWING
(ANONYMOUS, FOURTEENTH CENTURY)

T HE STORY OF CHRISTIAN'S CONVERSION IN *THE PILGRIM'S PROGRESS* BY
John Bunyan (1628-1688) is unforgettable. If you have not read the story,
let me summarize it for you.

Christian has been on the road a long time. His lower back aches. The
load he carries is getting heavier by the minute. Every step on this long
road seems harder than the last. And now—another hill to climb.

But this hill is different. As Christian grunts his way to the top, he spies
a cross. Just as he sees the man who hangs there, stubborn knots are

miraculously loosened and his burden falls off, tumbling down the hill into the mouth of a nearby tomb.

Christian is delighted beyond words. Tasting the liberating lightness of God's grace, he stands in rapt wonder at the foot of the cross. Tears stream down his cheeks. Three Shining Ones (members of the Trinity?) come to him with gifts: the promise of sins forgiven, new clothes to replace his rags, and a roll with a seal to present at the Celestial Gates. As his dazzling visitors leave, Christian leaps for joy and breaks into song.

It is surely a classic depiction of a conversion experience, a story that has woven its way into the fabric of the Christian imagination. More than two hundred years after *The Pilgrim's Progress* was published, Ralph Hudson penned the words of a popular revivalist chorus, "At the Cross." The echo of Christian's experience is unmistakable:

> At the cross, at the cross,
> Where I first saw the light,
> And the burden of my heart rolled away,
> It was there, by faith,
> I received my sight,
> And now I am happy all the day.

Crippling darkness gives way to light, cruel heaviness to ease, black despair to happiness. Life changes dramatically and irrevocably—all in that glorious moment of conversion at the foot of the cross.

Classic Conversion Stories

In the church circles in which I grew up, the importance of having a conversion story could hardly be overestimated. They were especially handy at campfires. "Testimony" should have been added to that list of indispensables—such as towels, sleeping bags and flashlights—that brochures insisted campers bring along.

As a boy of nine or ten (I write this with some measure of embarrassment as well as amusement) I actually stood up at a campfire on the last night of camp and made up a conversion story. Even at that age I was a veteran of campfires. Feeling the nearly palpable weight of communal expectations, I launched into a testimony. I modeled it on one I had heard before. I took that classic story of the man who reads John 3:16 and inserts his own name into the text, and I made the story my own—"For God so loved Mark . . ."

That was how, I explained to my fellow campers, I had become a Christian. True, it had never actually happened. But then again, it was a decent, believable story, and it made a positive impression on fellow campers huddled around the sacred campfire circle.

Yes, we are supposed to have conversion stories. Campfire times would be awfully dull without them. The problem was that I had no story, or at least no story I had been equipped to articulate, so I made one up. Like many others in my tradition, in spite of all its emphasis on a decisive moment of conversion, I had always thought of myself as a Christian. To put it another way, I could never isolate one pure and simple moment of conversion. My experience may well reflect the way the sovereign Spirit chooses to work in many people's lives. Unfortunately, it does not make for riveting testimonies.

I can look back on that experience now with amusement. But at the same time I find it troubling. I find it troubling because somehow I was given the impression as a young boy that if I did not have a dramatic—or at least interesting—testimony, my faith was inferior. Maybe it was even fraudulent. It was my own Catch-22. Not having a conversion story suggested a fraudulent faith. Making one up? Well that could hardly be better.

On the whole, I look back on the early years in my Christian community with profound gratitude. At its best the tradition I grew up in seeks to make the intensity of an initial conversion experience a paradigm for the ongoing process of conversion. But as much as I love the tradition and the simplicity of its clarion call to personal salvation, I cannot help but wonder if too often all the attention given to one decisive moment obscures the true nature of conversion. Obsession with the moment of conversion can blind us to the movement of conversion.

Conversion as Journey

Turn to *The Pilgrim's Progress* and it is remarkable how little attention Bunyan pays to Christian's conversion experience. It takes all of three paragraphs. Even before his conversion Christian is given every indication that his will be a life full of daunting challenges. He dreams of a stately palace, but only those willing to rush in and battle the armed guards will be able to stake their claim to its riches. Christian, in his dream, "not at all discouraged, fell to cutting and hacking most fiercely; so after he had received and given many wounds to those that attempted to keep him out, he cut his way through them all, and pressed forward into the palace." There a voice welcomes him, "Come in, come in; / Eternal Glory thou shalt win."[1] Bunyan's image of the Christian life is a long way from the cheery refrain, "and now I am happy all the day." Were *The Pilgrim's Progress* to be stocked in your local video store, it would not be found in the "Family Viewing" or even "Inspirational" sections. It is an "Action" flick, chock full of terror and violence.

There is nothing remotely static about Christian's life after his conversion. Most of the fascinating and transformative events in Christian's story happen after that burden tumbles down the hill. Far from being the end of his story, his conversion is the beginning of a life-shaping journey. After Christian's rapturous moment on the hill, getting beamed up to the Celestial City and its five star mansions is not an option. Instead he is thrown out on a rough road that happens to be the only way home. He is, after all, a pilgrim. Never fully at home, he is always on the move. While his travels take him to pleasant places (the Delectable Mountains and the Plain of Ease), sojourns in the Slough of Despond and the Mountain of Error are equally integral to his journey. So fraught with peril is Christian's way that others, his traveling companion Faithful confides, deridingly speak of "your desperate journey (for so they called this your pilgrimage)."[2] Every experience Christian goes through, delightful or terrifying, has its own divine purpose. As he hurtles from one adventure to the next, Christian is constantly being transformed. His progress as a pilgrim is dependent on his ongoing willingness to give himself wholeheartedly, unreservedly to the journey.

As contemporary pilgrims we may not have to fear the brutal thugs of Bunyan's Dead Man's Lane. But we face our own perilous journeys. Having heard the call of Jesus to take up our cross and follow him, he beckons every one of us to make our own interior journeys following in his way. Jesus journeyed to Jerusalem as the Son of Man called to lay down his life. Our road will also be a road of death. Never at ease with a world that crucified Jesus, never at ease with our own heart and its constant insurrection—we carry his very nails in our pockets, said Luther—we learn daily what it is to die to sin and self. But the road to Jerusalem is also a road of life. Like the Russian peasant in the spiritual classic *The Way of a*

Pilgrim, we journey to Jerusalem in order to venerate his life-giving tomb. Spirit-stirred, each day on the road we seek the place of our own new birth. Gradually the old is stripped away; the new is born. Above all, ours is a journey of transformation, of constant conversion. And the journey goes on.

Stages of Conversion

As for my own journey, it is ironic, given the fabricated scenarios of my campfire testimony, that just a few years ago I learned I did have a conversion experience. Apparently as a boy of five I came to my father and told him that I wanted to invite Jesus into my heart. I have no recollection of that moment, but I trust my father's word. What did it mean for me at five? I am not sure, but I suspect it meant everything it could mean at that age. According to Jesus, the faith of a child should never be dismissed.

Looking back, I draw deep consolation from the thought that somehow, beyond the reach of my understanding or even memory, God's Spirit was initiating in me his mysterious work of grace. Maybe that prayer of mine was the beginning of the journey. I have come to think of that experience as the conversion of my heart.

Seven years later, at twelve, I faithfully attended two weeks of nightly meetings on the topic of the Old Testament tabernacle. That may not sound particularly inspiring, but the itinerant speaker who came to our church brought along an impressive model. Accurate in every possible detail—the woods, the linens, the gold—it was a duplicate of the original. I was enthralled. The particulars of that preacher's teaching I do not remember. Decades later I admit to misgivings about all the fine points of tabernacle typology. But what I do remember is that God used those meetings to draw me into a fresh understanding of what Jesus' sacrifice on the cross meant. It had made my friendship with God possible. My eyes were opened, and I prayed and invited Jesus into my heart, partly because I was not sure if it had "taken" in the past and partly because I understood God's love for me in new ways, and it seemed right to respond. I think of that experience as the conversion of my understanding.

But it is one thing to understand your faith, another to live it. The contradictions and tensions of my adolescence made it all too plain that my faith was not taking hold of my life. I was doing the right things in my church life, but life at school among friends was a whole other world. I was living a divided life, and I knew God deserved something better.

When I was seventeen, on the last night of Senior High Camp the speaker called for a full commitment to Jesus. The message was deeply convicting and compelling. I was offered the prospect of a life of full-hearted devotion, a life in which all my fragments would find their true and simple center. I longed for that devotion and simplicity. After the meeting I walked out under the stars of a still August night and acknowledged Jesus as Lord of my life. This pledge has been in need of renewal every day since. During my subsequent senior year, tensions and contradictions did not miraculously evaporate, but their mastery over me had been successfully challenged. Jesus was Lord. I like to think of that experience as the conversion of my will.

And the journey goes on. Within a year, I was off to university to study political science and literature. Naturally my university years sparked questions about my faith. Did its claims stand up to thorough historical inquiry? Why was the tradition I grew up in so defensive about the arts and popular culture? It was a time of great learning. I read books at a pace I have never matched since. Writers such as C. S. Lewis challenged me to think as a Christian. At times, no doubt, I was too absorbed in the world of ideas, but I think of those years as the conversion of my mind.

Serious relationships were an important part of my early adulthood. Emotionally I found myself in deeper waters than I had ever been in before. Huge gaps in my emotional makeup were exposed. I was learning that it was not enough to do the right things and think the right thoughts. My inner person was in drastic need of an overhaul. (Ultimately, my wife would become my principal teacher.) I needed to confront honestly and painfully the emotional habits—rationalization, denial and secrecy—that were poisoning my inner life and hurting those around me. I look at those years as the conversion of my emotions.

After seven years of student ministry I was granted a sabbatical year. While its gifts were many, the greatest was a renewal of desire in my relationship with God. During that year I began to realize that for a decade I had been trying to satisfy my hearts' deepest needs for intimacy in the wrong places. That primal longing for God, that deepest desire, had been subverted and suppressed. A vague sort of guilt and inner restlessness took its toll on my spiritual life. Yes I could do the tasks of ministry. I could teach, I could lead. What I could not do was truly pray. At the deepest levels of my heart I had lost touch with God. My desires had subtly but surely shifted away from him. I had become a stranger to God, and as such I had become a stranger to myself. Thankfully, I was invited to renew my desire for God, my desire to know him and love him. I am still working out the implications of that year, a time I think of as the conversion of my desires.

There it is—a rough outline but still something of my conversion story. Of course, the real story is not nearly as neat and tidy as this compact retelling might imply. Stages of conversion invariably intersect and overlap. While God's Spirit has changed me in many areas—heart, understanding, will, mind, emotion and desire—I continue to need conversion in each, even though the Spirit seems to graciously focus his attention on one area at a time.

The story I have just told may be messier than that classic conversion story I felt obliged to tell as a young boy, but it has the merit of being a true story.

A Journey of Transformation

My journey is a rather ordinary one. It features none of the fireworks of those legendary testimonies. Nonetheless, it has been an adventure, an inner journey. Looking back, I see the patient hand of the Father tirelessly directing me through myriad experiences, all designed to change me, to help me shed false selves, to birth a new man in me. I wonder what God is up to now.

The road that Bunyan's Christian walks on is a road of ever-changing scenery. If there is one constant in Christian's pilgrimage, it is the constant of change. Faithful reminds Christian that those who obey the heavenly call should expect trials that "come, and come, and come again afresh."[3] After a grueling battle with the monster Appolyon, Christian continues on his journey, but with his sword in hand. As much as he craves rest, his time on the road has taught him that "some other enemy may be at hand."[4] While Christian's travels also take him to places of refreshment, these stays are invariably brief. The Plain of Ease is pleasant, but "quickly got over."[5] Great delight comes at the River of the Water of Life. Christian's weary spirits are enlivened by its waters. But it is not a place to camp: "They had not journeyed far but the River and the way for a time parted. . . . They were not a little sorry."[6] The solace Christian finds in the sweet and pleasant air of Beulah is but solace "for a season."[7]

In *The Pilgrim's Progress* either you are moving and going somewhere or you are going nowhere. Just as Christian leaves the Plain of Ease he encounters one of the few biblical characters that appear on his pilgrimage. It is Lot's wife. She is suspended in time, transformed into a pillar of salt. On the hard, right road Christian travels, there is no hope for those who look back and pine for what has been left behind. True pilgrims are "wayfaring men" gripped by "a desire to go forwards."[8]

Bunyan's classic tale invites us to think of conversion not so much as event, but as journey. Journeys have beginnings. Some of us know when our journeys began. But however dramatic the experience, it is only the beginning. Others of us do not know precisely when our journeys began. That should not be a source of anxiety. We do not question the reality of our physical life because we have no memory of our birth. Neither then should we question the reality of our spiritual life simply because we can not remember precisely how it all began. We are all on the road. How we got there is of relatively little importance. What is important is that we are pilgrims on a journey of conversion. Our hearts are pointed towards home. And the journey goes on.

Questions for Reflection and Discussion

1. What are the benefits and pitfalls of giving special attention to dramatic conversion stories?

2. Bunyan pictures the Christian life as a journey or pilgrimage. How does the image console you? How does it challenge you?

3. Do you find the idea of stages of conversion helpful? Why or why not?

4. How might you begin to sketch an outline of God's work in your life using the model of stages?

5. Looking at where God has taken you to bring you to this point in your pilgrimage, where is God doing his work of transformation now?

6. What can you do to give yourself more unreservedly and wholeheartedly to the journey?

TWO

TURNING OUR EYES ON JESUS
Julian of Norwich

Restore us, O Lord God of hosts;
let your face shine, that we may be saved.

PSALM 80:19

Believe me, all that thou hast sinned will be found pardonable if thou do not
blush to confess it. God awaits the sacrifice of confession from us that he may
accord to us the delightful boon of pardon. Accordingly, my dearest sons,
hasten to the remedy of confession. Lay open your wounds in confession that
the medicaments of healing may be able to take effect in you.

ALCUIN (C. 735-804)

Christ is a well of life, but who knoweth how deep it is to the bottom?

SAMUEL RUTHERFORD (1600-1661)

"TURN YOUR EYES UPON JESUS"—FOR SOME IT IS A FAVORITE HYMN. IT IS ALSO
sound spiritual counsel. Julian of Norwich, a deep theologian and a woman
of prayer, had some profound experiences of turning her eyes to see Jesus.
In *Showings*, written in the fourteenth century, she writes that lovers and
followers of Jesus will see him in three different ways. They follow a Lord
with three faces—a suffering face, a forgiving face and a glorified face.
According to Julian, at different points in our pilgrimages we will see these
three faces.[1]

The Suffering Face of Jesus
When we suffer, Julian suggests, we are invited to look into the suffering
face of Jesus. A good thing, surely, for we live in a world that can be a place

of unspeakable torment. Turn on the TV, read the newspaper—discover truth stranger and more perverse than any fiction. Witness the innocent three-year-old girl dragged off a suburban playground, brutally raped and murdered by a seasoned sex offender. Read reports of small aboriginal communities in northern Canada rocked by a reckless chain of suicides among their teenagers. Hear the trembling voice of a nine-year-old girl tell a reporter she saw her mother decapitated by neighbors in a spree of tribal violence.

Of course, pain is not just out there in the cold hard world of the media. It is an enemy that lurks in the corners of our private lives. Emotional wounds from our childhood can haunt and immobilize us. Family members, the very people we naturally look to for comfort and security, can wrench and break our hearts. Friends, lovers, even spouses can betray us, leaving us homeless in heart if not in body. In this broken world, pain can come from the most unexpected places.

Life is difficult for all of us, even for God's people. Our faith cannot protect us from the sharp edges of life and the mystery of suffering. For much of my Christian life I have been relatively free of serious doubt—a gift, not an achievement. But one question more than any other has troubled me as a believer—the age-old problem of pain. Why must our lives be so fragile, so vulnerable to pain, to tragedy, to sickness and death? This question presses on my spirit harder and more relentlessly than any other.

A few years ago my eldest daughter was sick with the flu. She blurted out to her mother, "Oh, Adam and Eve! Adam and Eve! It's all their fault! Why did they have to sin and ruin everything? I wouldn't have to be so sick!" Then she pressed my wife, "You know, really Mom, it's all God's fault. He knew they would sin and ruin everything. Why didn't he make them so they wouldn't sin?"

I cannot recall how my wife answered the question, but I have found no satisfactory answer for myself, at least no answer that fully satisfies my mind. But there is an answer. Faith does make a difference. To paraphrase the apostle Paul, we suffer, but not as others suffer. We suffer with hope, and while our suffering is real, so is our hope.

In fact, the most profound source of hope we have is found here in the first face of Jesus. Christians who suffer are able to look into the eyes of the suffering Jesus of the cross. This Jesus is a man touched with the feeling of our infirmities, a man who knows that we are made of dust, a man tested in all points as we are, a man of sorrows, acquainted with grief. He felt the torment of loneliness when closest friends deserted him. He wept in the face of death's power. He felt discouraged when so few understood his ways. There were times he felt confused over how to do the will of the Father in a twisted world. Mystery of mysteries, he felt the absence of the Father.

Jesus of Nazareth lived with nerves raw to the sharp edges of life. He asked the Father for no special clauses in his insurance policy. He wore no suit of armor. He is Emmanuel, not immune or indifferent to our pain but "God with us" in our pain. No other faith makes this claim of its God. No other faith offers such divine solidarity in our experience of suffering. And so I look into the suffering face of Jesus, and I find an answer that brings comfort to my heart and gives me strength to live on this pain-drenched planet. I have drawn immeasurable hope from the suffering face of Jesus.

The Forgiving Face of Jesus

According to Julian of Norwich, lovers and followers of Jesus are invited to look into the forgiving face of Jesus when they are sinning. If it is true that life is full of suffering, it is also true that as Christians we sin. Sin is another reality that presses on us daily. We hurt those we love most. We think thoughts we would never want to see exposed to the light of day. We make resolutions in the morning only to break them in the afternoon. We continually shatter the image of God that lies deep within us. We sin, and we do it daily. It is then, according to Julian, that we should see the forgiving face of Jesus.

But for many of us it is one thing to understand God's forgiveness, another to experience it. God's grace, expressed in the promise of forgiveness of sins in Christ, has always been central to my theology. But often that theology has not found its way into the center of my heart. Too often I have imposed my face onto the face of Jesus.

I believe that our relationship with God is as complex and layered and unpredictable as our deepest human relationships—in fact, more so. And as we grow in relationship with God, we bring patterns and expectations molded out of previous relationships, especially with those people closest to us. In my human relationships I have been sensitive, perhaps too sensitive, to the fact that my failures often meet with disapproval and judgment. I have hurt or disappointed others and have, in turn, felt their rejection. Because I have longed for acceptance, and at times have struggled with an inordinate desire to please people, it has hurt deeply to feel others' disapproval and judgment. Failure in our human relationships often creates mistrust, distance and guilt. In my life I have tended to impose this grid of human experience onto my relationship with God.

If I have sinned, I have displeased God, a God whose face I assume to be one of brooding consternation. As a result I have spent years dreading the honesty of prayer, dreading the obligation of daily confessing my sins to God. The honesty that confession calls for was too painful. When I repented, I felt no relief. I felt no new freedom. Instead I felt diminished and unaccepted. I felt judgment and recrimination. I was a failure in God's sight.

Theologically, I knew it was not supposed to work that way, but in the end, theological correctness was not enough. Pathways of the heart, beaten down by footprints of human relationships, had the final say in shaping the dynamics of my relationship with God. For ten years of my Christian life, prayer was agony. I feared its brutal honesty. I felt little forgiveness. I often simply stayed away from prayer. Thankfully, God has slowly turned me around. He has shattered inadequate images, initiating me further into the mystery of his love. In grace I have come to understand that confessing our sins is always a hopeful act. To confess our sins is to express confidence in God's goodness. It is his goodness that leads us to repentance. God receives no prurient pleasure in hearing the daily litany of our sins. Rather he asks us to be honest about who we are, to come clean and to take the first step on the way back to him. It is God who prompts our confession, and it is God who meets it with love.

Coming Back to Jesus

Julian of Norwich describes the meeting of persons that marks true confession: "And then our courteous Lord shows himself to the soul, happily and with the gladdest of countenance, welcoming it as a friend, as if it had been in pain and prison, saying: My dear darling, I am glad that you have come to me in all your woe. I have always been with you, and now you see me loving, and we are made one in bliss."[2] For Julian, confession in the end is reconciliation with our divine lover. The call to confession is not a call to warning or judgment but a call to love and pardon and hope. Even the pain of contrition, seeing ourselves for who we really are before God, is a gift to help us shed the deceptive soul-destroying ways of the past.

I began to see confession in this new light. God prepared new roads in my heart. Confession no longer left me mired in the failures of my past. It became a gift that opened me up to his good future. No longer a painful exercise that left me diminished and insecure, confession became an invitation to live in the security of God's mercy.

A few years ago God gave me a memorable experience of the forgiving face of Jesus. I was meditating on Luke 15, the story of the prodigal son. During my meditation I had one of those rare experiences when our whole lives are condensed and brought into the intensity of an encounter with God, moments when we stand before God seeing, with all the clarity we can imagine or bear, who we really are, where we have been, and where we are now—in the presence of God.

In that moment God gave me freedom to see that for years the yearnings of my heart had moved away from that primal desire to know and love him. While in the past I had been able to trace the consequences of misdirected desire in my life, in that moment I saw for the first time something of what those ten years of barrenness had meant to God. I began to feel some of the sadness the Father had felt as my desires had left him. I was the prodigal son who had squandered my inheritance. I had wounded the Father's heart. Turning back to the Father in my spirit and imagination, I fell into his outspread arms. Immediately I felt an overwhelming desire to pour recrimination on myself for failures of the past, for my selfishness and blindness. As much as I craved forgiveness, I had a stronger desire to hurt myself. But I kept hearing words from the Father, simple words: "I just want you back, Mark, I just want you back." Gradually, the desire to hurt myself subsided. I wept and let those words wash over me again and again. "I just want you back, Mark, I just want you back."

Jesus wants to cleanse us from our sins. He wants to free us from our past, to open us up to his new future. Jesus wants us to live under mercy in spite of our daily sins, to see his forgiving face. Jesus just wants us back.

The Glorified Face of Jesus

According to Julian of Norwich, most of the time in our Christian experience we are either suffering through hardship or waging battle with sin. It may not be an enticing portrait of Christian pilgrimage, but it has in its favor realism. It rings true. The hope hidden in Julian's portrait of Christian pilgrimage is that in our suffering, Jesus suffers too. In our sin Jesus is the one who forgives.

Julian suggests there is another face of Jesus that his lovers and followers will sometimes see. They may not see it often. But they will see it—the face of the glorified Jesus. How do we see this face of Jesus? There is no easy answer to this question. Even more than with the other two faces we need eyes open to spiritual reality. We need to cultivate spiritual openness in our hearts, an attentiveness to moments in our lives when the Holy Spirit gives us intimations of the glory of the life to come. These moments are not given to titillate our senses or to foster pride in exclusive spiritual experience. No, says Julian, we are given these moments because they stir up the faith and hope and love we need now to live as lovers and followers of Jesus.

One of the times the Holy Spirit seems to give glimpses of the glorified Jesus is when his followers are near death. No doubt it is these glimpses that allow so many Christians to die with incredible peace. But we do not have to wait until we are near death to catch glimpses of eternity, what Julian calls "sweet illuminations of the life of the Spirit."[3] Sometimes into the seeming ordinariness of our lives God gives us a foretaste of the glory to come. These moments may come to us now if we have eyes to see; in these moments we begin to see the glorified face of Jesus.

While my family was preparing for my year of study at Regent College, my parents, worried about whether our aging K-car could survive the rigors of a trip across Canada, graciously insisted we take their newer Pontiac. During that year in Vancouver my parents came to visit. When I picked them up at the airport, I wanted to be sure the car was in impeccable shape. I cleaned the dash, side panels, steering wheel, inside windows—everything except the inside of the rear window.

A couple of weeks earlier I had noticed the greasy print of a child's hand on the back window, barely visible in normal light. In fact when it came time to clean the windows, I could not find the small handprint. It only became visible when the light shone on it from a particular angle. Twice I had seen it as I drove down 16th Avenue with the sun setting brilliantly behind me. Caught in the light, that small hand print lit up into a blaze of gold. A little hand print, likely a mixture of popcorn butter and sweat, transformed into the hand of an angel, or at least a chubby cherub. It was dazzling, stirring. I had to remind myself to keep my eyes on the road ahead of me.

I was not about to declare my rear window the site of a sacred shrine, but then again, I was not about to wipe it off either. I need reminders that my three children bear "the weight of glory." Most of the time parenting consists of routine responsibilities—staggering out of bed at 5:30 a.m. to convince my son he should go back to sleep, driving my youngest daughter to her piano lesson on Monday afternoon, stirring up orange juice for my eldest daughter at the breakfast table. The list goes on, sometimes, it seems, interminably.

You might think that daily family devotions would faintly echo eternity in our home. In fact, they too tend to become part of the mundane, the routine. But a few weeks before my parents' visit, our nightly prayers had whispered rumors of glory. It was the night that we had finished reading *The Last Battle,* the final volume of C. S. Lewis's Chronicles of Narnia. We had a Narnian party at supper, then read the last chapter together, in which the main characters of the Chronicles are taken farther up and farther into the deep and wonder-filled levels of reality of Aslan's Land. Finally Lewis stops and explains that what happened afterward cannot be described in words. He can only say that what transpired was so real and so joyful that everything he had written in the first seven books was merely like the cover and title page of a big book.

We finished the chapter, shared our favorite Narnian stories with each other and said our prayers. My youngest daughter, who was six at the time, prayed, "Dear God, thank you for letting us read the cover of the book." It was a prayer that lifted the spirits of my wife and me at least as high as Lewis had. Did she hear an echo of eternity? The smear of grease became the hand of an angel.

It was a wonderful moment for us. But, alas, not the way life usually is.

Lest you think she is a precocious saint, just a few nights later when her turn came to pray, she chose the form of a primitive lament first developed by her older sister. It goes like this: "Dear God, thank you for a bad day. Amen." My son, who was lying next to me, sensed I was not entirely impressed. He whispered into my ear, "Daddy, that's the meanest prayer I've ever heard." For a child of three, no doubt exposed to horrendous amounts of blasphemy, this was no small claim!

My kids are like yours—like you and me—flesh and blood, often sources of frustration and weariness for those who care for them. But still the light shines in the darkness. We all, dim, dark and dull, bear the weight of glory.

I was not about to clean the rear window.

A Foretaste of Eternity

As I reflect on this chapter in our family life, I am reminded of the importance of being awake to the holiness of the ordinary, alert to Spirit-given glimpses of the glory. With eyes to see, they may flash forth in many ways. Perhaps these glimpses of glory come in the laughter of children or in their prayers. For many it is in the sheer and varied beauty of creation. It may be in other people that we catch glimpses of the glorified Jesus. Peter Kreeft calls our faces "souvenirs from Eden."[4] Somehow there we best glimpse the glory once ours that will be ours again, the Christ that plays in ten thousand places. Those married may see the face of the glorified Jesus most clearly in spouses, in the love and tenderness and forgiveness they mediate. Charles Williams writes, "In certain states of romantic love the Holy Spirit has deigned to reveal, as it were, the Christ-hood of two individuals each to other."[5]

We may have a foretaste of eternity as we join others in songs of worship. Music and devotion lift us beyond this world to the edges of the next. It may come in a moment of quiet, listening prayer. It may be when we eat the bread and drink the wine, and feel ourselves part of the feast to come. Whenever these moments come, the Spirit gives us them to treasure. We need to remember them, to celebrate them, to sanctify their place in our own sacred histories. If you are like me, these moments are rare. They are fleeting. We may find ourselves questioning their integrity. But they are very real.

To love and follow Jesus is to live under the deep enduring delight of his three faces. Jesus offers a hope that transcends the pain of our suffering, grants forgiveness in our struggle with sin, and wakens our primal longing for the joy that is to come. Then we will look full into his face, and know in our Jesus all shall be well, all manner of things shall be well.

Questions for Reflection and Discussion

1. In what way is Jesus himself the most profound answer to the problem of suffering and evil?

2. During times of suffering in your life, has Jesus seemed far away or close to you?

3. The forgiveness of sins is a central tenet of the Christian faith. How much is this truth an experience of your heart?

4. What are some of the obstacles that might hold you back from seeing the forgiving face of Jesus?

5. What kind of experiences give you glimpses of the glorified face of Jesus?

6. At this point in your pilgrimage which one of the three faces of Jesus do you need to see more clearly?

THREE

PRACTICING THE PRESENCE OF JESUS
John of Ruysbroeck

You hem me in, behind and before,
*   and lay your hand upon me. . . .*
Where can I go from your spirit?
*   Or where can I flee from your presence?*
If I ascend to heaven, you are there;
*   if I make my bed in Sheol, you are there.*

PSALM 139:5, 7-8

On earth there is so much concealment.

TERESA OF ÁVILA (1515-1582)

Knowing how to live one's life with Jesus is a great art; and knowing how to
hold him fast is the peak of wisdom.

THOMAS À KEMPIS (1380-1471)

I FELT AS IF THE MEETING WOULD NEVER END. IT WAS THE THIRD THREE-HOUR meeting of the day, and the theme of the conference was prophecy. The third consecutive speaker was about to begin. I was twelve years old and already bleary-eyed. My young soul had been saturated with prophetic truth. My parents were not oblivious to the taxing strain of these meetings on the young, so they had let me sit up in the balcony. There my nervous energy would be less distracting to others. I remember idling the time away by crouching down between the first row of seats and the balcony's front wall. My friend Larry had a small rubber ball. We both had pencils, and an improvised game of hockey began. It was one way to make it through the tediousness of those seemingly eternal meetings. It was also slightly more constructive though admittedly less fun than the diversion of other friends who shot spitballs from the balcony window onto unsuspecting pedestrians who walked below. Perhaps it is in part because of these less than pleasant memories of painfully long meetings that I have never been able to sustain much interest in all the elaborate intricacies of prophetic speculation.

Three Comings of Jesus

A few years ago a writer came to my attention who introduced me to the notion of three comings of Jesus. No, don't worry. I am not about to muddy the eschatological waters with yet another inventive spin. Far from being idle speculation bred in turn of the millennium hysteria, the notion of three comings of Jesus comes from the pen of a fourteenth-century Flemish writer, John of Ruysbroeck (1293-1381).

For Ruysbroeck the incarnation marked the first coming of Jesus. As he put it, in "the first coming He became man, for man's sake, out of love."[1] Ruysbroeck's third coming of Jesus is what we refer to as the second coming. But for followers of Jesus who live in between these two comings, our most appropriate focus is neither Ruysbroeck's first or third coming of Jesus. We need to look for his second coming.

What is his second coming? "The second coming takes place daily, often and many times, in every loving heart, with new graces and with new gifts, as each is able to receive them."[2] For Ruysbroeck the pressing question for a Christian is not how much historical investigation I have done into the first coming of Jesus, neither is it how much I know about the alleged signs of his third coming at the end of time. The pressing question for the Christian must be, how did Jesus come into my life, my world today?

But what about today? How has Jesus come into my life, right here, right now? Do I see the presence of Jesus in the smile of my wife who graciously forgives the tension I have brought into our home? Do I recognize his grace in my son's delight in growing thighs that enable him to scamper like a young colt on a soccer field? Do I hear the voice of Jesus in my reading of a biography that sparks questions and even dreams about my own life and family history? Do I see him in the witness of a member of my congregation who participates in a march of protest for the victims of AIDS? Do I see him in the faces of the poor and the needy? Where has Jesus come into my life today?

Cultivating Eyes to See

Ruysbroeck found himself gripped by Jesus' admonition to the disciples in Matthew 25:6: "Look! Here is the bridegroom! Come out to meet him." To begin practicing the presence of Jesus we need to look for what Ruysbroeck calls "the present coming of Christ . . . which takes place daily within our souls."[3] Seeing Jesus come into the fabric of our ordinary daily lives requires eyes that are wide open.

So often it seems as if I sleepwalk through my days. I lose myself and my sight in the rush and press of daily life. My eyes practice their own kind of self-fulfilling prophecy. I expect to see only the regular, the routine. And that is exactly what I get. I see nothing that stirs me, shakes me or wakes me up to the truth that Jesus wants to come into my life today. Annie Dillard writes that "seeing is . . . the pearl of great price."[4] Ruysbroeck, for his part, beckons us away from spiritual somnambulation into the attentiveness of what he calls the "God-seeing life."[5] Perhaps we need to begin each morning with the simple prayer, "Jesus, help me see your coming this day." At night, just before sleeping, we might take time to review our day, recalling those moments when we were aware of the presence of Jesus. Even these simple disciplines will take us a long way towards Ruysbroeck's "God-seeing life." We will become those who "make themselves ready" for the signs of his daily coming.[6]

One prayer I have used to make me more aware of the presence of Jesus is "the Jesus prayer": "Lord Jesus Christ, Son of God, have mercy on me, a sinner." Learning to quietly repeat this prayer in my heart as I go through my day helps me settle into an appropriate spiritual posture. I acknowledge who I am—a sinner in constant need of mercy. I also focus my attention on Jesus. Each word of address to him is theologically and relationally rich. I come to him as Lord, as Jesus, as Christ, as the Son of God. Each title accrues deeper meaning as I learn to make the prayer part of my very inner breathing. I have to confess that my own use of the Jesus prayer has been occasional. I have come nowhere near the experience of so many Christians who testify to its soul-shaping power. After years of disciplined use of the Jesus prayer, the anonymous Russian pilgrim of *The*

Way of a Pilgrim learned what it was to pray continually. The Jesus prayer became the beat of his heart: "Calling upon the Name of Jesus Christ gladdened my way."[7]

Creating a Valley of Humility

Recently I drove from Halifax, Nova Scotia, to my home in Wolfville, a small town nestled in the beautiful Annapolis Valley. I traveled along the oldest route in Nova Scotia. For centuries food has been transported out of the agricultural bounty of the valley to city dwellers on the rocky coast. The Annapolis Valley has a number of features that make it ideal for farming. For one thing, its soil, well drained on a sandstone bed, is rich and fertile. For another, its climate is less marine than most of Nova Scotia. The two ridges that rim the valley protect it from cold winds and heavy fogs that often assail the coastline. The valley itself acts as a kind of sun trap, collecting extra heat and energy from the sun. Add these factors together and we have what meteorologists call a *microclimate,* ideal for providing a rich harvest of fruits and vegetables.

According to Ruysbroeck, we can also invite the presence of Jesus into our lives by cultivating a sense of our own destitution without him. In so doing we create what he calls a valley of humility. Of course, attaining genuine humility is not easy. We are prone in our fallen nature to find security in the pretense of our own strengths. Our culture tells us that it is the self-reliant and self-confident who prosper. Many of us have been raised in the "age of self-esteem." In fact, these self-building strategies bring death to our souls. Simply put, those whose confidence is in themselves feel no need to look for Jesus to come into their lives. They feel no need to see Jesus; consequently, they often do not see him.

It may be helpful to remind ourselves that at his first coming Jesus came not to the high and mighty, but to pious God-fearing folk of the countryside. Mary received Jesus into her life as a humble handmaiden of the Lord. Her humility created a place for Jesus to come. It will be no different for the comings of Jesus into each of our lives. In the Sermon on the Mount, Jesus informs us that it is only the poor in spirit, the meek and the mourners, who will see the kingdom of God (and its King) break into their lives. Ruysbroeck tells us that the one who wants to practice the presence of Jesus needs to "take his stand upon his own littleness . . . [He] confesses and knows that he has nothing, and is nothing, . . . and when he sees how often he fails in virtues and good works, then he confesses his poverty and his helplessness."[8] In this confession we make our own valley of humility.

In making a valley of humility, Ruysbroeck tells us that we are emptied of self. We create a space where Jesus "shines into the bottom of the humble heart."[9] We create, as it were, our own microclimate. Our valley fills with his light. We bask in his heat, and our lives become fruitful with the knowledge of his presence. Even in our destitution we are consoled, knowing that Jesus never hides his presence from those who call out of weakness. According to Ruysbroeck, "Christ is always moved by helplessness."[10] Paradoxically, it is only when we squarely face up to the barrenness of life without Jesus that we begin to experience the delight of life in his fertile valley garden. W. H. Auden put it this way: "For the garden is the only place there is, but you will not find it / Until you have looked for it everywhere and found nowhere that is not a desert."[11]

Stretching Our Souls with Desire
We locals call them the North and South Mountains. Along the perimeter of the Annapolis Valley run two ridges. They are not really mountains. Visitors from the Rockies are bound to chuckle at the lofty designation we have given to ridges that rise seven hundred feet above the floor of the valley. Still, no one denies that it is impressive to view the valley from the edge of the ridges. Besides, they are our ridges, and we can call them what we want! Ruysbroeck suggests that the mountains that rim a valley remind us that just as souls must bow down in humility, so too they must stretch upward in desire. Practicing the presence of Jesus means rejecting a bland contentedness with the status quo. It means getting in touch with the painful rawness of our true condition—the destitution of our hearts, the desire that leaves our souls parched for the presence of Jesus. The psalms are full of this intense longing for God's presence: "As a deer longs for flowing streams, / so my soul longs for you, O God" (Ps 42:1). "My soul is consumed with longing / for your ordinances at all times" (Ps 119:20).

Likewise the early church eagerly anticipated the coming of Jesus at the end of time. You can hear the ache of expectant longing in the last prayer of the early church: "Even so, come, Lord Jesus" (Rev 22:20 KJV).

That same expectant longing needs to throb in the hearts of those who wish to meet Jesus as he comes into their daily lives. As a sense of our destitution creates a valley, a space for Jesus to come, desire for the presence of Jesus stretches the capacity of our hearts to receive him. Ruysbroeck assures us that when the soul "stretches itself with longing . . . it meets Christ, and is filled with His gifts."[12] Finding a phrase of aspiration from the Psalms and learning to repeat it quietly in our hearts will stretch our capacity for receiving Jesus. Perhaps "Even so, come, Lord Jesus" could be that constant prayer of desire.

Meeting Jesus in Unlikely Places

John of Ruysbroeck has given us some sage advice about practicing the presence of Jesus. As we look for the signs of his coming, we need to guard against the notion that Jesus comes most plainly into our lives during times of well-being and victory. Such is the force of his incarnation that he will grace even the most unlikely of situations with the knowledge of his presence.

One night during our family devotions we read Exodus 17. Israel has crossed the Red Sea. They are near the beginning of their trek across the desert. Already, barely in the wake of God's mighty act of deliverance at the Red Sea, they have established a habit of complaining about their present circumstances and looking longingly back to Egypt. In fact, just three days after the crossing, the griping begins. At Marah, bitter water leads to bitter spirits. God responds by sweetening the waters.

Israel is soon complaining again, though. This time their dissent is so intense Moses fears he will be stoned. And yet again, without a word of correction, God provides water. God may be extraordinarily patient in this narrative, but by this time Moses is weary of the roller coaster ride. He is fed up. He called the place *Massah,* which means "test," and *Meribah,* which means "quarrel." The Israelites had quarreled and tested the Lord.

Even as I began to read this story around our dining room table, I could tell things were not going to flow smoothly. There was a restless energy in the air. The kids seemed no happier than Moses to hear yet another story of Israel's complaining. A couple of times during the reading I had to stop and call for their attention. I was swiftly growing irritated.

After the reading came our regular time of questions and discussion. Things did not get any better. My son was off in that familiar hinterland between silliness and showing off. My eldest daughter persisted in fidgeting with the candles in front of her. I snapped at both of them. The admonition seemed to roll off them like water off a duck's back. They rolled their eyes, and again I spoke sharply. Finally, my youngest daughter responded to the tense situation by collapsing into a fit of giggles. That was enough. I was ticked off, and I sent her to her room.

After the questions came the closing prayer. I did not feel like praying. The atmosphere in our dining room was foul. I knew I had overreacted. I had mirrored the very lack of discipline of which I was accusing my kids. Facing the prospect of lifting my voice to God, I felt distinctly unworthy. The only hint of consolation I could find at that moment was that God had been faithful to his people at Massah and Meribah. I managed to squeak out a prayer. I thanked God for being with our family that night at our own Massah and Meribah.

Jesus is with us in all the petty squabbles and mean-spiritedness of our family life. We found ourselves that night in a place called "Quarrel," a place called "Test." Our behavior had been a test, not only to each other, but also to God. And yet in grace our family life goes on. Wounds are licked and healed. We give each other another chance. We try to love each other in our own peculiar, fitful ways. And Jesus is present in all.

We all wish our lives would be a journey from one high point to another, as if Israel could have moved from the Red Sea one day straight to victory at Jericho the next. We want our spiritual geography to be predictable, constantly elevated. For Israel it was not. For every Sinai there was a wilderness of Sin. For every burning bush there was a place of bitter waters. For every Jericho there was a Massah and Meribah.

So it is with my family. I feel great when family devotions flow smoothly, when some spark of spiritual curiosity is lit in the hearts of my children. I sense the presence of Jesus at work in our home. I am glad he is with us. But we have our share of the lands of Test and Quarrel as well. In a strange way it is even more consoling to know that Jesus is with us there too.

Jesus met us at our Massah and Meribah. In the Gospels he met the woman caught in adultery in the place of her humiliation. He met the disciples when they were cleaning their nets. Jesus stoops to meet us in the most mundane, the most shameful, the most unlikely places in our lives. Truly, as Ruysbroeck says, "He has sought us in strange countries."[13]

Marking the Second Comings of Jesus

A mature faith will be informed by all three comings of Jesus. Yes, we need to find our orientation in his first coming. The Word became flesh and lived among us. In his teaching, his living and dying, and living again, we find our bearing, our identity, our salvation. In the prospect of his future coming we find our hope, hope that will lighten even the darkest of days in these in-between times. In these two great moments Jesus enters redemptively into the sweep of human history. We live our lives within the grand contours of God's cosmic work of reconciliation in Christ. But it is in his "second comings" that Jesus enters redemptively into the sweep of our own personal stories in all of their uniqueness and concreteness. As Ruysbroeck notes, he comes so we "might taste Him in time."[14] In the unfathomable grace of God, you and I are invited to practice the presence of Jesus.

Questions for Reflection and Discussion

1. How does Ruysbroeck describe the second comings of Jesus in our lives?

2. How would you describe these comings in your own words?

3. Reflect back on the past twenty-four hours. Where have you seen the signs of Jesus' coming? Be as concrete as you can.

4. In what particular areas of your life are you prone to rely on yourself rather than on God?

5. How might such pride blind you to the coming of Jesus into your life?

6. What role does desire play in preparing hearts for Jesus' coming?

7. How has Jesus met you in the "Massahs and Meribahs" of your life?

8. What particular spiritual disciplines—those mentioned in this chapter or others—might help you practice the presence of Jesus?

FOUR

REACHING THE HIGHEST LOVE
Bernard of Clairvaux

Nevertheless I am continually with you;
  you hold my right hand.
You guide me with your counsel,
  and afterward you will receive me with honor.
Whom have I in heaven but you?
  And there is nothing on earth that I desire other than you.
My flesh and my heart may fail,
  but God is the strength of my heart and my portion forever.

PSALM 73:23-26

Who am I? This or the other?
Am I one person today, and tomorrow another?
Am I both at once? . . .
Who am I? They mock me, these lonely questions of mine.
Whoever I am, thou knowest, O God, I am thine.

DIETRICH BONHOEFFER (1906-1945)

It was through loving myself in the wrong way that I lost myself;
by seeking you alone and loving you sincerely, I have found both
myself and you.

THOMAS À KEMPIS (1380-1471)

B LAISE PASCAL ONCE SAID THAT THERE ARE TWO GREAT MYSTERIES—GOD AND ourselves. Of the second he writes, "What sort of freak then is man! How novel, how monstrous, how chaotic, how paradoxical, how prodigious! Judge of all things, feeble earthworm, repository of truth, sink of doubt and error, glory and refuse of the universe!"[1] Pascal is reflecting about the human condition in general, but even in our own individual lives many of us do have these wildly contradictory ways of seeing ourselves. Take the way I see myself. I can quickly offer two snapshots from my past, glimpses of tensions that inevitably affect and afflict the way I see myself. They both come from my adolescent years.

The Riddle of Self

In junior high school I was both popular and picked on. A good athlete, an easy person to get along with, I had many friends. But I was also very timid. I was not up to swaggering, name calling and swearing, the threats of physical intimidation that are critical in defining yourself as a young adolescent male. Fail to clearly mark out those defining boundaries and invaders will make their incursions. It made for a hellish early adolescence. Case in point: in my early teen years one of my friends announced that I had a head shaped like a peanut. Granted, my head is slightly on the large side. Two of my three children have inherited what my wife affectionately (I think) calls "the Harris head." Trust me, it is not grotesque. Still, back in junior high I endured a few weeks of being "peanut head." I remember looking in the mirror, tilting my head every conceivable way, trying to get a glimpse of what none of us can ever quite fully see—our heads.

To tell the truth, I could never find that peanut head, no matter how hard I looked. That should have been the end of it. *Dismiss the case of the alleged peanut head. Insufficient evidence. Throw it out of court. Get on with life.* That should have been the end of it. But it was not. In spite of plain evidence to the contrary, for a couple of years I walked around convinced that viewed from one angle, that one elusive angle I could not see (this made my fate more tragic), I looked more like that peanut-headed stick man on a bag of Planter's peanuts than the rather decent looking guy I saw in the mirror every morning.

Flash ahead a few years and I am in high school. Political science is my favorite subject, and I love to debate political issues. The highlight of my senior year is a trip to Ottawa, the capital of Canada. There I have the privilege of interviewing a former prime minister, the Right Honourable John Diefenbaker. The heady atmosphere of Parliament Hill only fuels my own political ambitions. I know what I want to do with my life—I want to be the prime minister. Sharing my dream with my classmates, my history teacher (should I bless her or curse her?) assures me that nothing will stand in my way. Brimming with self-confidence, ambition dripping from my pores, I am ready to take on the world.

Mark Harris, prime minister in waiting. It seems a long way from the raw insecurities of junior high. What happened to the peanut head? Unfortunately, he did not go away. He haunted the outskirts of my inflated view of self. At times he threatened to go public. At any moment, he could surface. It might be during a key political speech. Cheering crowds would see this promising political hotshot for who he really was—the Planter's peanut-headed stick man. Not your average political scandal, but surely catastrophic to cherished political aspirations.

I can look back now over twenty years later and laugh at the blatant internal contradictions I lived with. (Laughing at myself, I have gradually discovered, is an important spiritual discipline.) Anyone who knows me now would find the idea of my desire to be prime minister laughable. And I can thankfully report that it has been well over twenty-five years since anyone has informed me that my head looks like a peanut. (Are people just getting more polite?) But don't get me wrong. At midlife there is still a prime minister and a peanut head lurking in my self-consciousness. Just scratch slightly underneath the surface of this apparently well-adjusted, solid citizen and you will find the same blatant contradictions. It is not that I think too much of myself, or too little. I still routinely do both. In the words of John Newton, which I have embraced as my own, "I am a riddle to myself; a heap of inconsistence."[2]

Ultimately all our attempts to define ourselves, to forge a stable self-image, are theologically wrong-headed and doomed to failure. At best we construct impressive facades with flimsy foundations. Psychologists tell us that there are a number of options in the world of self-esteem.[3] I can have a weak self-image (read: vacillating between peanut head and prime minister) or a strong self-image (read: the fixed consoling delusion that I am either the peanut head or the prime minister but not both). I can have a negative self-image (read: peanut head) or a positive self-image (read: prime minister). The problem is that none of these options are adequate self-images for followers of Jesus. All of them are self-definitions, and as such inherently skewed and unhelpful. Heaps of inconsistencies, all of us, we desperately need some authoritative outside help to get a true sense of who we are.

Four Levels of Loving God

Perhaps no one in the history of the Christian church has more to say to people who struggle to see themselves accurately than Bernard of Clairvaux (1090-1153). Bernard was a towering figure in the life of the medieval church. Although he was a political adviser to kings, a gifted administrator and spiritual leader of a thriving monastic order, above all Bernard was a lover of God. In his treatise *On Loving God* Bernard writes with profound insight about the way we see ourselves and its intimate relationship to the way we see God.

According to Bernard there are four levels of loving God. The first level of love is the love of self for self's sake. Bernard is thinking not of calculating self-interest or preening narcissism but of the basic impulse all healthy human beings have to look after themselves. When I get up in the morning and pick up a razor, I intend to shave the stubble off my face, not to slit my wrists. Jesus assumes this instinct for self-love when he charges his disciples to "love your neighbor as yourself" (Mt 19:19). Bernard seems to be suggesting that without this basic instinct to care for and value ourselves, we would have no basis for learning to love others or God.

Bernard's second level of love is the love of God for self's sake. At this level, human beings look beyond themselves and call out to God for his help and protection. But note, at this level we call out to God not because we love him but because we need him. I remember as a young Christian when I first became vividly aware of how thoroughly my devotion to God was polluted with self-interest. Even in my moments of confession (the clearest evidence I could find of self-denial), I realized I was turning back to God essentially because I was miserable. Restored fellowship with God felt a whole lot better for me. That was long ago, but years later I remain painfully aware that my confessions are often shot through with self-interest, what Bernard calls the love of God for self's sake. I still pray with the Anglican poet John Donne for "a repentance, not to be repented of."[4]

Being honest about our propensity to self-interest, however, should not lead us to despair. Bernard assures us that God can lead us into a higher level of love—the love of God for God's sake. Jonathan Edwards, the great Puritan, offers this bracing challenge to a self-absorbed faith:

> What chiefly renders God lovely, and must undoubtedly be the chief ground of true love is his excellency; yea it is his infinite beauty, brightness, and glory itself. . . . If men's affection to God is founded first on His profitableness to them, their affection begins at the wrong end; they regard God only for the utmost limit of the stream of divine good, where it touches them and reaches their interest, and have no respect to that infinite glory of God's nature which is the original good, and the true fountain of all good, the first fountain of all loveliness of every kind, and so the first foundation of all true love.[5]

Reaching the third level of love, we are among those who Bernard says trust in the Lord "not because he is good to [them], but simply because he is good."[6]

To this point reaching the highest love seems to entail a letting go of self and a fuller preoccupation with God. It comes as something of a surprise then when Bernard suggests that the highest level of love turns us back to the love of self—but with a huge twist. The fourth level of love is the love of self for God's sake. Bernard is advocating a way of seeing ourselves that is deeply rooted in our relationship with God. There is, he suggests, a love of self that is not the self-preservation of the first level but a higher, chastened love of self, fueled by love for God and a zeal for his glory.

Accepting God's Radical Redefinition

I feel as if Bernard is talking about a level of love well beyond my reach. Frankly, I find it hard to love myself when so often I feel that internal exile that every human feels, as a stranger in the strange land of self. How can I be expected to love this self, so slippery and foreign? If ever predictable, it predictably falls short of even my own expectations, let alone God's. How can I be expected to love a self so consistently disappointing?

Each of us has weaknesses, constitutional defects in our temperaments, wounds, that are a source of great inner anguish and shame. These wounds not only torment our inner lives, they also lead to attitudes and actions that deeply hurt others. Often those we love are hurt most grievously. The sins of parents are passed on to children, generation after generation (Ex 20:5). When I was young, this was simply a memory verse. Now I understand it as a poignant insight that captures so much of what is tragic about our human existence. This cycle of wounding spins on, and we all have a place on its wheel. Our wounds also make it difficult for us to imagine that level of love that Bernard writes of, where we love ourselves for God's sake.

If there is any wound in my heart that debilitates me and the growth of my faith more than any other, it is a wound of timidity. I lack courage. Put me in a place of conflict and my emotions seize up. I just want to get out. I have no idea how to express my opinions with passion or clarity. In order to minimize the threat of disagreement, I instinctively align myself with a response that maintains the peace. It might be the right response, it might be the wrong response, but it is the only response I seem able to muster within. I am a peacemaker to a fault. I will gladly lose myself and my own convictions to maintain the peace.

Some time ago I had to mediate in a sharp conflict between two of my friends. The deepest feelings of two people I cared about were at stake. This situation forced me to trust my own gut convictions. I am embarrassed to report that I could not find those convictions. Instead, I instinctively opted for the alternative that offered the greatest possibility of maintaining the peace. Maintaining the peace, a false, fear filled peace, was my gut(less) conviction. In the end it was my own personal peace that I was trying to protect and not the best interests of my friends. I lay awake that night haunted by my reaction, a reaction that echoed countless other such reactions in the past. I had failed to find a place of courage and conviction, groping my way instead to an easy, hollow compromise. I felt spineless, even selfless. As I lay in bed I found myself hoping there was another me inside, capable of acting with courage and conviction. I also reckoned I did not know that self, the self I hoped to be, longed to be. There seemed no way even to touch that self, not even the hint of a path that might help me find it. That night I felt the grip of a black terror, an abyss—not the horror of who I was but the horror of who I was not, nor could even imagine myself ever being. It was profoundly disquieting, a dark place from which only the light of prayer could lead me back.

And pray I did. I prayed that someday I would find that self I was supposed to be, that self I could touch now only in the grim haunting specter of what I was not. In the end the Spirit helped me turn away from paralyzing self-doubt. I did not turn away in denial. The darkness was there. The light of God's Spirit did not dispel the darkness so much as confirm its presence. But what I did receive from the Spirit was what I could not find within—hope. The Spirit assured me that he knew where this new self was, that as he had brooded over dark chaotic waters and birthed an orderly and beautiful creation, so too he would brood over my darkness and create a new self. He called me to trust him with the birthing of a new man. I received no immediate answer, only a deep and hopeful promise, but that was enough. It got me to sleep that night.

I do not always live so intensely with myself. I do not and I should not. But what this experience illustrates for me is that in large part my salvation rests on my faithfulness in making this turn away from futile attempts to define myself, this turn towards God, to find hope in his radical redefinition of who I am.

Grounding Our Identity in Jesus

Our growth into Bernard's fourth level of love, the love of self for God's sake, means being deaf to voices of self-adulation and self-loathing, voices that leave us confused and insecure, hopelessly absorbed in a culture of self. We come to an end of ourselves. Pascal puts it this way:

> Know then, proud man, what a paradox you are to yourself. Be humble, impotent reason! Be silent, feeble nature! Learn that man infinitely transcends man, hear from your master your true condition, which is unknown to you.
> Listen to God.[7]

Listening to God, his Spirit whispers true, objective words into my thin and tangled subjectivity. He tells me that I have been created by a loving Father, nurtured with unstinting divine care since the moment of my conception. Not only has he given me myself, but in Jesus Christ he has given me himself. In the face of my waywardness and wretchedness (this too is part of who I am) he has given his very life for me. Now that I have thrown in my lot with Jesus, the Father sees me in him.

While we are given only tantalizing clues as to how Jesus came to understand himself and his special destiny, we do know that Jesus grew in wisdom (Lk 2.52). Presumably he experienced that growth in self-understanding that every human being experiences. Isn't it interesting that just as Jesus is about to begin his public ministry the Father speaks to him with words of deep assurance. As John baptizes Jesus, Jesus feels the waters of the Jordan streaming down his face back into the river, and he hears the Father's voice, "You are my Son, the Beloved; with you I am well pleased" (Lk 3:22). The Father's love is communicated to Jesus in a powerful way. His divine sonship is uniquely affirmed. Secure in his identity, Jesus heads off to do the work he has been sent to do.

To be a follower of Jesus is, in some sense, to follow his path of self-understanding. Paul tells us that our lives are hidden in Christ (Col 3:3), and so are our identities. Hidden in him, we hear the Father whisper, "You are my beloved daughter" or "You are my beloved son." In grace the Father tells us who we are—hopeless sinners, infinitely loved—and he holds out hope for who we will become. We trade in our fraudulent, insecure self-identities for our strong and true identities as children of God. Swept up in Christ into the mystery of intimate relationship with the Father, we shed our self-important ego-centeredness and begin to see ourselves in a new, awe-inspiring light as the beloved. Bernard writes, "In [my creation] he gave me myself; in [the incarnation] he gave himself; and when he did that he gave me myself. Given and given again, I owe myself in return for myself, twice over."[8]

Living in the security of his love, receiving the radical redefinition of his grace, we are free to respond to that love by offering ourselves for all that we can be to him. We open ourselves in order to be a place where his purposes can be expressed, where his glory can shine. We love the self that he desires us to be. Secure in this new self, we are free to laugh with equal lightness at the voices of self-adulation and self-loathing. We can live, like Jesus, a self-forgetful life in service to God and others, a life in which we find, and even love, ourselves. Freed from the prison of self, we love ourselves for God's sake.

Home to Self, Home to God

I must confess that I have experienced very little of this love. I take some consolation from the fact that Bernard himself wondered if it was possible to fully experience this fourth level of love in this life. I do know, though, that among the sweetest things I have ever tasted are those rare moments when I have been graced with the freedom to forget myself—in worship and in service to others. Perhaps in those selfless, God-centered, redefining moments I have trudged on the outskirts of Bernard's fourth level of love. However fleeting these moments have been, I am supremely grateful for them. They have given me a hunger for more. They have pointed my heart in the right direction. One day I will make that turn away from self and towards God for the last time. No longer seeing through a glass darkly, I will know, even as I am known. I wonder what it will be like? Bernard writes, "I have no doubt this is how it will be when the good and faithful servant is led into the joy of his Lord. . . . It will be as though in some miraculous way he forgets himself and . . . comes wholly to God, and afterward holds fast to him, one with him in spirit."[9]

Questions for Reflection and Discussion

1. John Newton wrote, "I am a riddle to myself; a heap of inconsistence." How do you relate to Newton's sense of frustration?

2. What is the ultimate problem with our attempts at self-definition?

3. Bernard of Clairvaux writes about the four levels of loving God. What is the main level out of which you seem to operate?

4. What are some of the wounds in your heart that make it hard to love yourself?

5. What does it mean that our new identities are grounded in Jesus?

6. What does it mean to accept God's radical redefinition of our identity? How might you open up your heart to allow God to do this work?

OBSTACLES
ON THE JOURNEY

Some travelers never make it to their destination because they are unprepared for obstacles they encounter. Too often these obstacles leave pilgrims frustrated or disoriented, resigned to making little or no headway. Spiritual dryness, prayerlessness, temptation and discouragement can make us wonder whether it is possible or worthwhile to stay the course of Christian pilgrimage. John Newton, Origen, the Desert Fathers and Evelyn Underhill assure us that there is a way through these obstacles. More than that, these masters of the spiritual life invite us to understand that, approached rightly, these obstacles have the potential to move us forward on the hard but joyful road of Christian pilgrimage.

FIVE

WORKING THROUGH SPIRITUAL DRYNESS
John Newton

If I say, "Surely the darkness shall cover me,
* and the light around me become night,"*
even the darkness is not dark to you;
* the night is as bright as the day,*
* for darkness is as light to you.*

PSALM 139:11-12

In a certain sense, aridity can almost be taken as a sign of progress in prayer,
provided it is accompanied by serious efforts and self-discipline.

THOMAS MERTON (1915-1968)

You say in your letter "below everything, I believe I'm in a way very quiet and
happy"—well, that, not the fluctuating surface moods represents your true
spiritual state, and is the work of God. Give Him thanks for it and trust it and
don't bother about the variable weather.

EVELYN UNDERHILL (1875-1941)

OUT MY OFFICE WINDOW I SEE A DAMP, OVERCAST DAY—A DISAPPOINTING DAY, especially when October days in Nova Scotia can be magnificent. There is nothing quite so invigorating as a bright sunny day at this time of year. A sharp but still pleasant coolness is in the air and everywhere you look is the blaze of autumn colors. It is disappointing then to look out on a gray day.

Then a second look challenges my lazy assumptions. As I look out again I notice that the leaves outside my window are striking. Green maple leaves mellow into a deep plummy yellow. Brilliant oranges mingle with fiery reds. Instead of being obliged to reflect the blinding stare of sunlight in the dazzling but sometimes distracting play of light and shadow, on this dark day these leaves shine with an inner radiance, silently celebrating luminous colors they claim as all their own. Free from the sharp light of the sun their colors are all the more clear and resplendent. They glow with that mysterious inner light that Rembrandt evokes in so many of his portraits. So an apparently dreary day offers me its own peculiar gifts, as long as I am truly willing to look. Careful observers of the spiritual life have long observed similar dynamics at work in the seasons of the soul.

Seasons of the Soul

John Newton (1725-1807) is best known as the reformed slave trader who wrote "Amazing Grace." What is not so well known is that in addition to penning many hymns, Newton was also a prolific letter writer. As Newton rose to prominence from his pulpits in Olney and London, men and women from all over England wrote to him seeking spiritual counsel. He responded with letters full of wisdom and warmth and a winning transparency about his own limitations. In one of those letters, addressed to "Mrs. W.," Newton is particularly eloquent, encouraging her to consider the value of all the seasons of the soul, especially those hard, dry seasons that seem at first glance to be anything but gifts:

> These [seasons], like fits of the tooth-ache, though troublesome, are not mortal. . . . They are like winds to the trees, which threaten to blow them quite down, but in reality, by bowing them every way, loosen the ground about them, circulate the sap, and cause them to strike their roots to a greater depth, and thereby secure their standing. If a tree were to grow all upwards, and the roots not to enlarge in proportion to the branches, it would be laid flat upon the ground by the first storm. It is equally unsafe for a believer to be top-heavy; and therefore the Lord suits and changes his dispensations, that, as they increase in gifts, knowledge, judgement, and usefulness, they may grow downwards likewise, and increase in humility. Since we have been enabled to put ourselves in his hands, let us stand to our surrender, and leave him to carry on his work in his own way.[1]

Newton is writing about seasons of dryness that come to Christians as a matter of course, dry seasons that paradoxically strengthen our faith.

But seasons of dryness are not always from God's hand. Sometimes we make choices that invite dryness into our souls. Masters of the spiritual life have long pointed out that failure to confess sin will create deadening distance in our relationship with God. As with any intimate relationship where we wrong a friend and then try to pretend that nothing has happened, the understanding whispers of friends give way to the awkward silences of mere acquaintances.

The Danger of Unexpressed Anger

Unexpressed, even unconscious, anger towards God can have the same effect. It is almost inevitable that there will be times in our lives when we will feel anger towards God. After all, we believe that God is ultimately in control of our lives. When we feel angry or disappointed with life, we are likely to feel angry or disappointed with the Lord of life. The problem for many of us is that we have never been given permission to express our anger. We have been taught that such honesty is arrogant, even blasphemous. As a result, we bury our anger in the hidden recesses of our hearts. But like a deposit of lead at the wellspring of a fountain, that anger will surely and steadily poison our intimacy with God. Unspoken, even unrecognized anger, invites stiffness, then silence, into our relationship.

A simple exercise that I have profited from during seasons of dryness is writing a prayer to God that begins with the word *why*. Take pen to paper and let the hard questions come out. At times I have started the exercise with no idea I had any pressing questions that needed articulation. Gradually, as I have begun writing, I have been surprised by both the number of questions and the intensity of feelings that have risen to the surface. Coming clean with those questions and the anger they articulate has had a purging effect on my relationship with God. Nothing is hidden. Everything is on the table. All is in place for a fresh start in my journey of intimacy with him.

Our anger needs to be dealt with head on. Like the psalmists of the Old Testament, we need to take our anger into prayer and express it in all of its fury and rawness. God is more than capable of handling our anger, and it is in his presence that anger is most likely to be transformed into something creative.

Unconfessed sin and unexpressed anger, then, are two classic cases where we can wittingly or unwittingly invite seasons of spiritual dryness into our lives. In such cases God may seem a remote figure. Prayers may rattle not just off the ceiling but off the very top of our skulls, not because God has withdrawn himself from us but because we have withdrawn ourselves from him. To get things right, to restore intimacy, we need to humbly make our way back to God.

The Strange Gifts of Dryness

In his deeply insightful letter to Mrs. W., Newton has another sort of season of spiritual dryness in view. This season is actually sent to us from the hand of our loving Father. Though a struggle to endure, Newton insists such seasons can bear strange rich gifts for the willing, trusting recipient. I certainly have experienced these times of dryness and, in some measure at least, can witness to their ultimate usefulness.

One thing God seems to be doing in these seasons of dryness is training us in the school of charity. I am using charity in the original sense of the word—self-giving that has only the needs of the other in view, and asks for nothing in return. Most of the time in our spiritual lives we are receiving from God. We are aware of his goodness, the many gifts he showers on us through friends and family, creation and his word, learning and art, Christian community and the sacraments. In short, most of the time we are receiving from God.

These seasons of receiving are good. They are to be enjoyed and celebrated and remembered—remembered because while seasons of receiving are good, they are also seasons. By their very nature they come and go. During seasons of spiritual dryness, when our hearts are heavy, our spirits dull, when God seems ever so far away, we are being asked by the Spirit not to receive, but to give. We are being asked to offer our obedience, even our devotion, not because of what we get out of it, not because it is the first impulse of our hearts, but because he asks us to, and because he is more than deserving of any of the gifts we bear.

In seasons of dryness God teaches us how to give. We are in his school of charity, and if your spirit is half as guarded and miserly as mine, there is nothing you need to learn more than disciplines of charity. It is all too easy for me to be sharp and critical in my relationship with my wife and children. Recently I noted in my journal, "It is frightening, really, to know how petty I am capable of being. Lord, lead me to a place in my spirit that is more generous." Seasons of dryness, responded to properly, can lead us to that place. Schooled in the ways of charity in our primal relationship with God, the capacity for charity forged in this divine-human crucible will pour out into the rest of life, into our relationships with family members, friends, neighbors and strangers. Seasons of dryness are God's chosen classrooms.

Strangely enough, at the very time that we feel not even a slight impulse to pray, when every well of desire to pray has dried up, it is most important that we do so. Why? Because we desperately need to learn how to forget ourselves and to give, because these prayers, stripped of vividness and passion as they are, register as prayers of great value to God, prayers that come from a deep place within us that responds to God even in the experience of our own barrenness. These prayers are not the gifts of a young lover drunk with the pleasures of love, ultimately more absorbed in the love he experiences than in the lover. Instead they are the gifts of a seasoned lover who gives for giving's sake, for the good of the beloved. In such giving we reflect back to God that divine charity he lavishes on us, and surely his heart is warmed.

Seasons of dryness have the merit then of freeing us from a relationship built largely on the dubious foundation of our emotions. By consistently deferring to emotions in our spiritual lives, we will inevitably fall prey to the petty despotism they impose. We will love God when we feel like it, and ignore him when we feel like it. We will spend Sunday in a state of near spiritual ecstasy, and grow cold and indifferent in the harsh realities of Monday. Our relationship with God will bear all the restless, troubled unpredictability of a young adolescent crush. Guided by the inconstant moon of immature lovers, our devotion will ebb and flow.

Growing Deeper with God

We all know that any human relationship based on emotions and only emotions is a fragile construct at best. If, for example, my relationship with my wife were to be principally dependent on the way I feel about her, our relationship would be in trouble. It is true that at times I feel passionately about my wife. I feel the surge of romantic love, the mystical sense of oneness that is one of marriage's greatest gifts. Such feelings are not to be slighted. They have inspired poetry and song for millennia. But like all feelings, feelings in marriage come and go. The feeling of romantic love simply cannot be sustained. I think I am much like other husbands in that sometimes I wake up in the morning, look across the bed at my wife, and in my stupor and foul spiritedness I feel very little for her. (I am sure that she could say the same for me.) Far from feeling the delight of romantic love, I may find myself hard-pressed to discover any positive feelings whatsoever. What do I do then? If I am at all mature in the ways of love, at that point I will choose to love my wife. I will choose to be kind, thoughtful and courteous. Not because I feel like it but because I know that to act in such ways is what is good and right, regardless of how I feel. Kindness, thoughtfulness and courtesy are also what my wife deserves, so when the feelings of love stop, it is time for the disciplines of love to begin. These disciplines are built not on the inclinations of emotion but on convictions of the mind and commitments of the will.

I have also noticed something curious in my relationship with my wife. When I give myself over to the disciplines of love, when I choose to treat her with the honor and devotion she deserves, gradually, almost imperceptibly, the embers of desire are stirred. I do not know exactly how it happens, but the magic and the passion, the flame of romantic love, returns. Romantic love brings it own delights; it also has the effect of spurring me on, fueling my efforts in the disciplines of love. It is good. But in and of itself, romantic feeling will not sustain mature love.

Surely a similar dynamic is at work in our relationship with God. Seasons of dryness will come. This is the unanimous witness of saints from biblical times through to the present. When the pleasant buzz of emotion goes, when spiritual delight is a fading memory, it is time for the disciplines of love to stretch their muscles. It is time to allow spiritual disciplines to be grounded in our minds and wills, time to doggedly and consistently pray and listen to the Word, not because we feel like it but because it is good and right, and we know in our heart of hearts that God deserves such honor and devotion.

In grace God sends these seasons of dryness our way to free us from the superficiality of a relationship that will remain stunted as long as emotions are permitted to impose their childish fascism. To use John

Newton's metaphor, God is asking us to sink our roots deeper in the soil, a reaching downward that ultimately makes possible a stretching ever upward. It is God who graciously dispenses the seasons of the soul, and while seasons of fecundity are obvious gifts to be joyfully received, seasons of dryness too can come from his hand bearing strange hidden gifts.

Newton writes these wise words of admonition:

> Rejoice . . . that ye are God's husbandry. The early and the latter rain, and the cheerful beams of the Sun of Righteousness, are surely promised to ripen your souls for glory;—but storms and frosts likewise are useful and seasonable in their places, though we perhaps may think we could do better without them. . . . Both are needful to perfect our experience and to establish our faith.[2]

Ours is to trust him in all the seasons.

Questions for Reflection and Discussion

1. John Newton reflects about the different seasons Christians experience (seasons of sunshine, seasons of frost and storm). Try using the language of seasons to describe your own spiritual state. In what kind of season are you now?

2. Review the quotation from Newton's letter to Mrs. W. What value does he see in seasons of dryness?

3. Unexpressed anger is a common cause of spiritual dryness. How much freedom do you feel in expressing your anger toward God?

4. With reference to our fluctuating moods, Evelyn Underhill advises us, "Don't bother about the variable weather." How easy or hard is it for you to follow her advice?

5. In your experience what are some of the strange hidden gifts in seasons of dryness?

6. How would you characterize your love for God? Is it based on romantic feelings, disciplines of the will and mind, or both?

SIX

COMBATING PRAYERLESSNESS
Origen

Come, bless the Lord, all of you servants of the Lord,
   who stand by night in the house of the Lord!
Lift up your hands to the holy place,
   and bless the Lord.

PSALM 134:1-2

The raising of the hands in cross-vigil, that is the word of the hands, and the word of the eyes, moreover, it is the raisings of them up to God, and the word of the knees and of the legs is the sending of them in prostration, and the word of the body, moreover, is when it is extended to God in prostration.

NINTH-CENTURY CELTIC GLOSS ON PSALM 133

I needed peace and silence to give free play to this quickening flame of prayer.

THE WAY OF A PILGRIM
(ANONYMOUS, NINETEENTH CENTURY)

FEW HAVE LIVED SUCH DRAMATIC LIVES. AT AGE SIXTEEN, ON FIRE FOR HIS faith, Origen (c. 185-c. 254) sought martyrdom. Only a determined mother, who hid all his clothes and so prevented him from leaving the house, saved him. A few years later, pursuing chastity, anxious to avoid even the hint of scandal in teaching female converts, he mutilated himself. While Origen proved to be a brilliant teacher, the greatest theologian of his age, he was banished from his hometown by his bishop. He was also to suffer imprisonment and torture. After his death, church synods labeled him a heretic for some of his unconventional views.

Origen would hardly seem like the person to look to for sane, practical advice on the life of prayer. Curiously enough, though, that is exactly what we find when we open the pages of his treatise "On Prayer." He begins this work by acknowledging that even to begin to speak of prayer is to skirt the edges of a great mystery. Origen recognizes the spiritual heights we are daring to ascend when we talk about prayer: "The discussion of prayer is so great a task that it requires the Father to reveal it, His First-born Word to teach it, and the Spirit to enable us to think and speak rightly of so great a subject."[1] To speak of prayer, then, is to broach the mystery of the triune God. We are on holy ground.

Preparing to Pray

Standing on holy ground, as Moses discovered, requires its own spiritual etiquette. Origen begins by admonishing us to pay attention to the way we prepare ourselves to pray. Too often my own efforts in prayer have floundered and sputtered because I have failed to pay proper attention to the need for adequate preparation. I rush straight from a world of frenzied activity into the presence of God, and then wonder why my thoughts are so distracted and chaotic, why it is so hard to concentrate on prayer. I have forgotten to ready myself for "the great transition," I have neglected the rites of preparation prayer demands.

If we stop and think about it, our lives are full of these rites of preparation. At breakfast this morning I did not begin my meal by opening the refrigerator door, grabbing the orange juice and drinking it straight from the container. No, the orange juice had to be poured into a glass. Tea had to be brewed. Bread was toasted golden brown, then covered with a swath of delicious maple butter. The toast was placed on a plate, then carried, with the tea and orange juice, into the dining room. There I sat down, prayed, and then ate my breakfast. Rites of preparation made it possible for me to enjoy my breakfast. Preparing to write this morning I searched files and bookcases, spread appropriate resources over my desk, found the pen and paper I wanted and sat down; then I could begin to write with a measure of focus. In so many areas of life, whether we are conscious of it or not, we enact rites of preparation.

These rites are no less important when we begin to pray. Think about the transition we make. We leave a world of noise and speed to search for a still, quiet center; we move from a world where human agendas and actions are given priority into a world where God's agenda and actions must be given first place. It is not an easy transition. It should not be made glibly or presumptuously. Origen suggests that "the person who is about to come to prayer should withdraw for a little and prepare himself, and so become more attentive and active for the whole of his prayer." Preparing ourselves, Origen tells us, is a way of clothing ourselves before we present ourselves to God, for "it is impious to approach Him carelessly, sluggishly, and disdainfully."[2] According to Origen, preparing to pray may mean letting go of anger nurtured in our hearts and asking for grace to forgive. It may mean taking a few quiet moments to let go of the clutter of thoughts that preoccupy us and to focus instead on the greatness of God, to "peer beyond the created order and arrive at the sheer contemplation of God and at conversing with Him reverently and suitably as He listens."[3] Ideally, the one who prays aspires to "forget for the time being everything but the prayer he is praying."[4]

How do we prepare to pray? What clothes do we put on to enter the presence of God? What helps us shed our scatteredness and find a simple center in God? I suspect our answers may differ. For some a vigorous walk releases the tension that has slowly seized our muscles. As we walk we move from a preoccupation with our thoughts to a preoccupation with God. For others it might be listening to the medieval plainsong of Hildegard of Bingen or the choruses of contemporary praise music. Perhaps it is quieting our hearts through devotional reading. We will each clothe ourselves for prayer in our own distinctive ways, but if we hope to get anywhere in our prayer lives we need to discover those rites of preparation that work best for us, and we need to practice them with diligence. These simple rites have the potential to lure us into the presence of God. In practicing these disciplines of readiness we are, according to Teresa of Ávila, laying bait for our souls, summoning our hearts to an attentiveness that opens them wide to the work of God's Spirit.[5]

Dealing with Distractions

When all is said and done, even with the most appropriate rites of preparation our prayer lives will not be totally free of distractions. Wild careening thoughts and sometimes repulsively malignant thoughts will come our way, taking our focus off our prayers. What do we do then? Some masters of the prayer life recommend pulling the distraction into our prayers. For example, if I find myself thinking about that vacation I would like to take, I should quickly bring that desire to God and ask him for his discernment, then get back to the regular rhythm of my prayers. At times I have found this approach helpful. Perhaps the best approach to dealing with distractions is simply to call ourselves back to attention by addressing God: "Lord, here I am, with my thoughts wandering. Help me keep my thoughts focused on you." Know that God understands our limitations, and move on in prayer. Don't allow the distractions themselves to become a distraction.

The reason so many of us battle with distractions in prayer is that we live distracted lives. We are distracted at work, distracted when we are with our friends or families. Our inner world is rarely composed and serene; however, if we are willing to persevere in prayer through the distractions, God will give us a gift that may well enrich other areas of our lives. If I learn to spend ten minutes intently focused on my conversation with God, giving him my full attention, I am also far more likely to be able to bring a new measure of focus into the rest of my life. I will listen without distraction as a friend or family member pours out his or her heart to me. I will focus my attention on each of life's tasks, giving myself fully to each moment as it comes along. Striving for a less distracted prayer life, then, has the potential to lead me into a less distracted life in general.

A Call to Embodied Prayer

As we have seen, Origen is careful to acknowledge the great mystery that is prayer. Paradoxically, he insists that we need to begin our thinking about prayer with feet planted solidly on the earth.

After the first flush of some intense spiritual experiences in my teen years, I found myself genuinely puzzled. Why, if I was created for spiritual communion with God, did he choose to fetter me with a body that seemed to impose severe limitations on my devotion? At the very least I needed to eat regularly and to clothe my body daily, and I wasted nearly a third of my day in the apparent uselessness of sleep. It did not make sense. Compared to the yearning ache of the soul for God, the taste of eternity in the heart, I could not help but see my adolescent flesh as cumbersome at best, a locus for demonic distractions at worst. Looking back, the question seems embarrassingly naive, but that tendency to denigrate the flesh and exalt the spirit can be a constant temptation for those who pursue the spiritual life. We need to remember the incarnation, the Word became flesh. We need to think through the glorious implications for our own bodies. As the fourteenth-century Orthodox theologian Gregory Palamas wrote, the incarnation has "made the *flesh* an inexhaustible source of sanctification."[6] The body has a central place in prayer.

If we think of prayer first as elevation into sustained celestial song, we will likely find ourselves singing the prayerlessness blues. Surround our image of prayer with gorgeously plump, rosy cheeked cherubs and we will likely feel the wax of our own wings melt as we take an Icarus-like plunge. Any realistic understanding of prayer needs to take into account that prayer is the response of our whole person—spirit, mind and body—to God. Origen understands that effective prayer begins with attention to our bodies.

Specifically, Origen suggests the position of our bodies in prayer demands consideration. Posture is not the preoccupation only of mothers and teachers who zealously corrected our slouches; posture is important in prayer. Origen recommends that one posture is particularly effective: "The hands outstretched and the eyes lifted up is to be preferred before all others, because it bears in prayer the image of characteristics befitting the soul and applies it to the body."[7] His point is simple. The posture of our bodies can give expression to the impulses of our souls. But perhaps his argument can be taken further. It seems to me that not only can our souls lead our bodies, our bodies can also lead our souls. Stretch out your hands, lift your eyes to heaven, and let flesh school spirit into aspiration and concentration, a steadfast looking beyond yourself to the God of your salvation.

When it comes to posture there are many options. Origen notes that when we confess our sin, kneeling might be the most appropriate posture. I remember a student telling me that he liked to kneel when he prayed because kneeling was something he did for no one else, a gesture of reverence and devotion, a language of the body reserved only for the intimacies of his relationship with God. I often pray seated in an upright alert position, hands turned open at my side. Sometimes I begin a time of prayer with deep breaths, consciously letting go of the anxieties and preoccupations that clutter my inner life. Sitting, kneeling, dancing, lying face down on the ground—all may be appropriate responses of the body to grace. If we are serious about prayer we need to pay conscious attention to posture; to put it in contemporary language, Origen is calling us to embodied prayer, to praying unapologetically and freely with our bodies.

Place and Prayer

If posture is important in prayer, so is sense of place—where we pray. Obviously it is important to acknowledge that prayer can take place anywhere. As Origen writes, "Let it be known that every place is suitable for prayer if a person prays well." But the freedom and flexibility we have to pray anywhere should not blind us to the merits of having a specific place where we regularly pray: "But everyone may have, if I may put it this way, a holy place set aside and chosen in his own house, if possible, for accomplishing his prayers in quiet and without distraction."[8] Some places are simply too noisy and laden with potential distractions to be considered as places for concentrated prayer. If we suffer from even the slightest perfectionist impulse, prayer near a cluttered desk or in a messy room is a highly unlikely proposition. Origen goes on to note that other places disqualify themselves from consideration because they have taken on some negative associations, such as places where we have committed sin or places of painful memories.

But if some places discourage prayer, that is all the more reason to seek out places that draw us into prayer. Origen suggests that "prayers in the churches . . . have something exceptional for the person who assembles in them genuinely."[9] The stillness and the rich symbolism of a church sanctuary may prime our spirits for prayer. Praying in church also has the salutary effect of reminding us that, at best, our private prayers flow out of our prayers together when we gather as a community of God's people.

Of course, praying regularly in church sanctuaries is not a realistic option for many of us. My own mornings often begin with a walk through my backyard to the church where I have a study. Here my day starts with prayer. So often, even as I approach the door to my study, I am conscious of the many times God has graced me with a sense of his presence in that room. The door is opened. Light pours in through the windows, and memories of meeting God are heavy in the air. A desire to pray is stirred in my heart. For other people it may not be a particular room but a walk along a familiar path or sitting down in a special chair. I have a friend who finds that a bathtub is the best place to meet God. Distractions are at a minimum. Tensions are relaxed. Prayer can flourish. As with posture, so with place: there is no right or wrong answer. We need to seek solutions that fit the peculiarities of our own situations.

Perhaps our prayer lives have been areas of struggle. Perhaps our relationship with God is in need of renewal. Attention to rites of preparation, posture and place have the potential to rekindle the flame of prayer. Our care in attending to these preliminary details signals to God the intensity of our desire to know him and love him. Knowing that his desire for intimacy with us is overwhelmingly stronger than our own, we can be confident that he will meet the feeble stirring of our desire with the tender strength of his own. For Origen the preliminaries are important. There is no point in aspiring to stratospheric dimensions of prayer until our feet are planted firmly on the ground. As in so many other areas of life, if we truly want to get ahead, we need to begin by getting back to the basics.

Questions for Reflection and Discussion

1. Do you think it is necessary to set aside special times to pray? Why or why not?

2. What rites of preparation for prayer do you use?

3. What are the most common distractions in prayer that you struggle with?

4. What strategies for dealing with distractions have you found most helpful?

5. How much freedom do you feel to pray with your body?

6. What sort of postures or gestures do you use?

7. What sort of places draw you into prayer?

8. How may these places become part of your regular discipline of prayer?

SEVEN

RESISTING TEMPTATION
The Desert Fathers

Therefore let all who are faithful offer prayer to you;
at a time of distress, the rush of mighty waters
*   shall not reach them.*
You are a hiding place for me;
*   you preserve me from trouble;*
*   you surround me with glad cries of deliverance.*

PSALM 32:6-7

To soothe that he may hurt is the way of the devil.

JOHN CHRYSOSTOM (C. 334-407)

Temptations—these have always been the stepping-stones by which the Saints marched forward.

THOMAS À KEMPIS (1380-1471)

E VEN THE STRONGEST OF CHRISTIANS KNOWS WHAT IT IS LIKE TO BE TORmented by temptations. A recognized master of the spiritual life, Thomas à Kempis nonetheless felt worn down by their steady assault:

> That is what often distresses me and shames me [Lord] in your sight; that I am so apt to fall, so weak in resisting my passions. Even though I don't give way to them all together, the way they keep on at me all the time is very irksome and distressing; I get sick and tired of living day in, day out, at war with myself.[1]

I think Thomas à Kempis speaks for all of us. Whoever we are, suburban homemaker or university student, young professional or retired senior, we find ourselves caught in the crossfire of this battleground.

Over the course of our lives, the face of our temptations may well change. The visceral temptation to lust that fires the groin of a young man changes as he reaches middle age. While the temptation to lust after younger women can still be strong, it is less physical and more spiritual. Troubled by signs of his own inevitable aging, the middle-aged man ultimately seeks not the pleasure of flesh on flesh but the hope of eternal youth, the false promise of eternal life. He does not want to grow old. More to the point, he is afraid to die. The face of temptation changes, but temptation itself never goes away.

Desert Warriors

In the third and fourth centuries thousands of men and women left cities and villages and headed out into the deserts of the Middle East. In large part it was a protest movement. They were sickened by a lax spirit of accommodation that permeated the life of the church. This occurred around the time that Constantine officially recognized Christianity. Christians no longer lived with the fear of persecution. In fact, it became a cultural imperative to give at least some sign of lukewarm allegiance to the new faith. These desert fathers and mothers knew that Jesus called his followers to a purer discipleship. In the desert they hoped to genuinely live out the call of Jesus to sell their possessions, leave all and follow him.

But the desert was to hold surprises for those men and women. They abandoned the city hoping to say good riddance to its alluring temptations and slippery compromises. It would not be so easy. They discovered that it was one thing to leave a city and its prostitutes behind. It was much harder to leave the temptation to lust behind. If anything, the force of lustful thoughts seemed to intensify in the harsh light of the desert. The desert was to become a spiritual battleground. Some of the consistent victors in these battles became men and women prized for the wisdom they dispensed to those younger in the faith. Their pithy sayings and quirky stories are still charged with spiritual insight.

The Gift of Temptation

The story is told of young monk John who prayed to the Lord to take away all his passions. Having seemingly become invulnerable to temptations,

John strode in to visit one of the elders of his community, confidence dripping from his voice. "You see before you a man who is completely at rest and has no more temptations."

The elder replied, "Go and pray to the Lord to command some struggle to be stirred up in you, for the soul is matured only in battles." The young monk left a chastened man. "And when the temptations started up again John did not pray that the struggle be taken away from him, but only said: 'Lord, give me the strength to get through the fight.' "[2]

The story of this young monk contains an element of surprise designed to jar us out of spiritual complacency. I must confess I have never felt compelled to ask the Lord to stir up new temptations. I have more than enough old ones. But the point of the story is that God can use temptation in our lives. Perhaps we have allowed ourselves to think that spiritual maturity is marked by invulnerability to temptation. In fact, spiritual maturity is marked by consistent victory in the experience of temptation. It is only in the heat of the battle that the strongest spiritual mettle is forged.

Another wise elder, Abbot Pastor, said, "The virtue of a monk is made manifest by temptations."[3] Temptations can be a gift. Abbot Pastor notes that when we resist temptation it can be a great source of encouragement. Perhaps we are prone to dwell on compliments, allowing them to sow thoughts of self-promotion. Then one day, after a raft of compliments come our way, we realize that we have managed to take them in stride. We have kept steadily on a humbler course. Old patterns of sin that once held us are loosening their hold. Temptations that once haunted and taunted us we can now resist. We have learned to utilize some of the resources of our faith, and God is at work creating in us a new heart. This progress is worth celebrating. Temptations can be a gift. They make manifest our virtue.

Last year I found myself experiencing something of this new strength. It was an encouraging time. In my journal I wrote about "a new quality of resistance to temptation—not a stronger sense of resolve as much as a more focused and faith-full looking to Jesus."

But if one benefit of temptation is its potential to reveal new areas of strength, I was to learn that temptations can also temper any illusions we have of our own invulnerability. Perhaps a spirit of self-congratulation had crept into my heart, but the strength I had experienced collapsed just a few weeks later. I found myself in a pitched battle with old temptations. Deeply

ingrained patterns of sin I naively imagined had been put to rest rose
fiercely and malignantly to the surface.

It was discouraging. Gradually, though, I came to recognize that while
temptation can reveal new areas of strength, it can also steady us, tempering
exaggerated self-confidence. Temptation was a strange gift, pointing out
to me in my blindness areas of my own heart still in desperate need of
transformation. Blinds opened up. Light poured in on dark and dusty
rooms, rooms I had neglected, rooms of which I was simply unaware. It
was as if Jesus said, "Mark, here is a place in your life in desperate need
of attention. Learn to let go of the old ways. Die to them. Open yourself
up to the new work I want to birth in you." I have heard Jesus speak these
words to me in the past, and I will likely hear them again in the future.
And when I hear them I know I am at the beginning of a long journey. It
does not feel like it will be easy. But it does feel like it will be good.

Discerning the Ecology of Temptation

While the desert fathers help us see that temptation can be a gift, they also
provide us with sharp insight into how we can resist temptation. One of
the consistent teachings of the scriptures regarding temptation, implied in
the narratives of Joseph and David and made explicit in the teaching of
Paul, is simply to flee it (1 Tim 6:11; 2 Tim 2:22).

A brother came to Abbot Pastor, deeply troubled about frequent and
intense assaults of temptation. The abbot led him out of his cell into the
open air and said, " 'Open up the garments about your chest and catch the
wind in them.' But [the brother] replied: 'This I cannot do.' So the elder
said to him: 'If you cannot catch the wind, neither can you prevent
distracting thoughts from coming into your head. Your job is to say No to
them.' "[4] There is nothing sinful about being tempted. Abbot Pastor
reinforces the truth that temptations are resisted most successfully when
we deal with them at their earliest stages. Even in entertaining the seduction
of a temptation we are surrendering something of ourselves to it. Our
resistance is weakened. Better to simply say no at the first opportunity.

One of the keys to fleeing temptation is discerning what leads us there
in the first place. If we are vulnerable to acquisitiveness, buying things to
dull the ache of inner emptiness, then casual trips to a nearby mall are
obviously not a good idea. We need to flee temptation. James Houston

calls this process "discovering the ecology of our sin, then choosing to move in the opposite direction."[5]

We need to ask ourselves some hard questions. What are the typical external conditions or internal emotional configurations that invariably make us vulnerable to temptation? I once went through a period in which I irresponsibly lashed out in anger towards my children. The ferocity of my reaction was hardly justified by the circumstances. Why was I flying off the handle? When I scratched a bit deeper into the stuff of my heart, I began to see that my unwarranted anger at my children was actually rooted in anger I felt at someone else who had hurt me deeply. What did I do then? I needed to recognize and acknowledge that wound of pain. Better to muster the courage to feel that pain than to let the anger it festered explode at innocent bystanders. I came to understand that when I felt the swell of that pain and anger within, it was time to ask God for help. Talking to a good friend was also part of my healing. In taking these concrete steps I was able to discern the ecology of my sin, and I began moving in the opposite direction. I fled temptation and invited the work of grace into my heart.

Seeing Temptation's Lie

In order to be vigilant in resisting temptation in its early stages, we need to see through its seductive illusions:

> Another of the elders said: "When the eyes of an ox or mule are covered, then he goes round and round turning the mill wheel; but if his eyes are uncovered he will not go around in the circle of the mill wheel. So too the devil if he manages to cover the eyes of a man, he can humiliate him in every sin. But if that man's eyes are not closed, he can easily escape the devil."[6]

The elder's point is clear. Fail to see temptation for what it really is, and we will find ourselves servile slaves of sin, trudging in well-worn footpaths of the Evil One's design. Here the desert fathers are calling us to brutal honesty with ourselves and God. Yes there is a momentary rush in a fix of pornography. But the plain demands of truth call us to see beyond the seduction to the high costs of pornography to the soul—the shame, the self-loathing and, most tragically, the diminished capacity for that true intimacy our hearts crave.

Or let's take the subtler case of jealousy. There have been times when I have been jealous of one of my friends. He exudes ease and grace in social situations. People warm up to him quickly. I am invariably more reticent. I can come across as somewhat stiff and aloof. It is easy for me to be jealous of my friend's social abilities, easier still to think of my jealousy as a relatively innocent vice. But no, I need to see through its lie. If I give that jealousy play in my heart, a spirit of resentment will gradually poison my friendship. My capacity to celebrate my friend's strengths will shrivel. I will grow blind to my own unique God-given gifts. I will end up seeing my friend and myself for less than we truly are in the sight of our loving Creator. Resisting temptation requires steely vigilance in ferreting out its lies and half-truths. We need to have our eyes wide open.

Taking the Offensive in the Battle

The desert fathers are not content, though, with simply being on guard against temptation. They want us to take the offensive in this spiritual warfare. Like many Canadians, I am a passionate fan of hockey. One of the most unnerving experiences for a fan is seeing your favorite team build up an early lead and then retreat into a defensive shell. So often it is an invitation to disaster. The best defense, after all, is a good offense. It is a principle that holds true in those battles for the possession of our souls.

Ultimately, the best strategy for resisting temptation is a positive one. Unlike most desert fathers who were peasants, Arsenius came from an aristocratic background. While still in the royal court he called out to the Lord for salvation. "And a voice came saying to him, 'Arsenius, flee from men and you will be saved. . . . Flee, be silent, pray always, for these are the source of sinlessness.' "[7] Staying close to God in our daily living is the best preparation for battle. Take time to get away from the wearying pace, the pervasive distractions of the daily grind. Carve out space for solitude; spend time in quiet and prayer. Take the knowledge of God's love and presence into your days as you live a life of intimate fellowship with God. Be his faithful lover. These are the sources of sinlessness.

Finding Victory in Jesus

Abbott John's advice was simple, but in the end it might be the most important:

A monk must be like a man who, sitting under a tree, looks up and perceives all kinds of snakes and wild beasts running at him. Since he cannot fight them all, he climbs the tree and gets away from them. The monk, at all times, should do the same. When evil thoughts are aroused by the enemy, he should fly, by prayer, to the Lord, and he will be saved.[8]

Like the monk in Abbot John's story, we should be terrified by our capacity for sinning. There is no point in looking to ourselves for help. Instead, we look to Jesus. Temptation again becomes a peculiar gift. It drives us to Jesus, to look away from our weakness to his perfect strength. It is in him, and only in him, that we will secure our victory.

Recently my ministry was publicly slighted. I was hurt. In the days that followed it was all that I could do to fight off critical and spiteful thoughts. In the end I found that my greatest defense was simply calling out to Jesus. By calling on his name, the hurt I felt was put into perspective. Jesus knew far more about being maligned than I ever would. But Jesus did not demean my feelings either. I felt his assurance that he was with me in my struggle. Meditating on his gracious response to enemies pulled my heart out of spitefulness and set me on a road to forgiveness. Calling on the name of Jesus made all the difference.

Jesus is our defender. We remember that the one who was tempted in all points as we are is now the perfect high priest who prays for us in our weakness. He is now the risen, exalted Christ. Called to share in his life, his power is at work in us. The liberating force of his new creation has been unleashed. Facing temptation we instinctively and resolutely look to Jesus. We trust in his victory and participate in it. Armed with the shield of his victory, we brandish a spirit of profound hopefulness as we battle temptation. Thomas Merton notes that "the practice of keeping the name of Jesus ever present in the ground of one's being was, for the ancient monks, the secret of the 'control of thoughts,' and of victory over temptation."[9]

A Burning Passion for God

The desert fathers saw themselves as spiritual athletes, training and disciplining themselves in the life of the spirit. Perhaps Abbot Lot was tempted, like our contemporaries who work out in weight rooms with wall-to-wall mirrors, to sneak yet another self-admiring glance at the pleasing new definition in his spiritual muscles.

> Abbot Lot came to Abbot Joseph and said: "Father, according as I am
> able, I keep my little rule, and my little fast, my prayer, meditation and
> contemplative silence; and according as I am able I strive to cleanse my
> heart of thoughts: now what more should I do?" The elder rose up in
> reply and stretched out his hands toward heaven, and his fingers became
> like ten lamps of fire. He said: "Why not be totally changed into fire?"[10]

Abbot Lot learned that it is not enough to take pride in a scrupulously
guarded life. Mere victory over temptation is not enough. Instead God calls
us to radical transformation. Richard Rolle, the English medieval writer,
writes that "the perfect never carry combustibles with them into the next
life! All their sins are burnt up in the heat of their love for Christ."[11] What
a notion! It is love that consumes sin, not conscience, theological
correctness, moral rectitude or the fear of punishment. Love for Christ is
that positive burning force that resists temptation. I am not one of Rolle's
"perfect"; I am not even close. Still, I find it to be a compelling vision of
the life of holiness. It is love for Jesus that spurs us to resist temptation,
burning away our very will to sin. Perhaps Augustine said it best: "To my
God a heart of flame; . . . to myself a heart of steel."[12]

Questions for Reflection and Discussion

1. An abbot advised John: "Go and pray to the Lord to command some
struggle to be stirred up in you, for the soul is matured only in battles." What
point is he trying to make?

2. According to the desert fathers, how can temptation be a gift?

3. What are the typical temptations that assail you?

4. What is the lie hidden in these temptations?

5. What strategies do the desert fathers suggest for resisting temptation?

6. Which strategy might be most helpful for you?

7. What can you do to cultivate a spirit of hopefulness as you battle
temptation?

EIGHT

OVERCOMING DISCOURAGEMENT
Evelyn Underhill

The Lord is my light and my salvation;
  whom shall I fear?
The Lord is the stronghold of my life;
  of whom shall I be afraid?

PSALM 27:1

Let these beginners not grow weary but trust in the Lord that, if they pray and do what they can for themselves, His Majesty will make them in very deed what at present they are only in their desires.

TERESA OF ÁVILA (1515-1582)

And because of His visitation, we may no longer desire God as if He were lacking: our redemption is no longer a question of pursuit but of surrender to Him who is always and everywhere present. Therefore at every moment we pray that, following Him, we may depart from our anxiety into His peace.

W. H. AUDEN (1907-1973)

T HERE HAVE BEEN TIMES WHEN I HAVE WANTED TO GIVE UP. SPIRITUAL BATTLES I was fighting were the same old battles. Little ground had been won or lost. Fierce resolutions to change withered in the face of stubborn habits of the heart. Glaring contradictions between my lofty ideals and my lowly practices became like a stench in my nostrils. The more I thought about it, the more I sank into discouragement.

Thankfully, I do not allow my feelings of discouragement to become the debilitating force they have been in the past. One writer who has helped me immeasurably in my struggle with discouragement is Evelyn Underhill. Underhill was born in England in 1875 into a family with little interest in religion. Nonetheless, her studies in philosophy, her fervent interest in the lives of the saints and, finally, an overpowering vision led to her conversion when she was in her early thirties.

In 1911 her book *Mysticism* was published. It became a classic in its field. Later in life, though, Underhill expressed some reservations about the work that had established her reputation. The subtitle of the book, *A Study in the Nature and Development of Man's Spiritual Consciousness,* hints at what in hindsight she would see as the book's principle weakness. She had viewed mysticism primarily through the lens of human religious experience. In her "Preface to the Twelfth Edition" (1930), she commented that if she were to rewrite the book, she would give more emphasis "to the predominant part played in [the soul's] development by the free and prevenient action of the Supernatural—in theological language, by 'grace.' "[1]

God's Prevenient Grace

As her own Christian faith deepened, Underhill discovered that the starting point of her spiritual life was not her own quest for higher levels of spiritual consciousness. Rather its starting point was God and his gracious initiative in her life. In a letter to a friend, she wrote,

> Is it not amazing when one can stand back from one's life and look back down on it—or still more, peep into others' lives—and see the action of the Spirit of God: so gentle, ceaseless, inexorable, pressing you bit by bit whether you like it or not towards your home? I feel this more and more as the dominating thing—it seems so odd that everyone does not feel and notice it happening, don't you think?[2]

Underhill was experiencing the tender yet relentless press of God's grace. Her conviction concerning the priority of grace in religious experience was reinforced when she met the great scholar and spiritual guide, Baron von Hügel. Underhill never downplayed her debt to this man. In 1929 she wrote a letter in which she questions the notion of religion as an evolutionary quest of the human spirit. After a warm and affirming opening she challenges her correspondent, quoting von Hügel:

You *should* face the fact that "Christ as the ideal which in the course of human evolution man may become"—is not Christianity. Christianity says that in Christ God *comes to man*—enters the time process. As von Hügel says somewhere "the essence of religion is *not* development from below, but a golden shower from above."[3]

That golden shower was God's prevenient grace.

Baron von Hügel had insisted that the prevenient grace of God was the antecedent of religious experience. Prevenient grace means that God is always moving ahead of us, taking initiative in our lives, wholly independent of our own worthiness or, for that matter, even our aptitude for discerning evidence of his grace. It is simply God's way to gently poke and prod us forward even in the face of our obtuseness. He acts, he invites, he beckons, he calls for our response. It may be through scripture or prayer, through preaching or the sacraments. It may be through the ordinary events of our lives—circumstances, conversations or inner thoughts. Whatever means he may choose, he invariably lays out a path for us to walk in and offers his hand of guidance. It is not that we have no part in our spiritual growth. Ours is to discern, to listen, to develop a sharper eye for God's initiatives and then to respond with increasing sensitivity and resolve to the direction in which his prevenient grace points us. Our will is crucial. But it is ever and always God's grace that leads the way.

Underhill's eventual espousal of the priority of grace did not make her any less astute as an observer of religious experience. More than being attentive to the complexities of religious consciousness, now she was being attentive to the very work of God and its effects on the human soul. It is not surprising, then, that like her mentor von Hügel, Underhill became a prized spiritual director to many. In her *Letters* she consistently encourages correspondents to trust in God's grace.

The Seduction of False Humility

Trusting God's grace means taking our eyes off setbacks that tempt us to quit. Discouragement can be difficult to resist. It seduces us with its smoky alto voice. In the same way blues singers gain a peculiar sense of consolation in documenting all their ills, Christians can derive a perverse pleasure from a spiritual masochism that continually berates the self. After all, we tell ourselves, we are being honest about our flaws. We are courageously looking them straight in the eye. Others may flinch or deny their darkness. We do not. We know how truly weak and inadequate we are. And the faintly disguised voice of a subtle pride, a false humility, prattles on. Underhill is insistent that we make a sharp distinction between self-disgust and true humility: "Instead of wasting energy in being disgusted with yourself, *accept* your own failures, and just say to God, 'Well, in spite of all I may say or fancy, this is what I am really like—so please help my weakness.' This, not self-disgust, is the real and fruitful humility."[4]

To another correspondent apparently prone to navel-gazing and self-flagellation Underhill advises,

> You've got to get rid of that obsession of sin, you know; it's a crudeness, an inferior sort of humility at best—and really rooted in disguised self-occupation! I've had it badly so I know all about it. Look at Christ and not at yourself. Regard the inclination to useless remorse as a temptation. There is not much to choose between the best and the worst in us, seen in the spiritual light, is there? Just let the love of God wash over the whole thing. It's the only Christian attitude.[5]

Underhill is not for a moment downplaying the importance of genuine remorse. What she is taking on is a "useless remorse" that shows itself fraudulent by leading us to absorption with ourselves instead of God's pardoning, hopeful grace. To another correspondent bit by the same snake, she writes, "Though humility and acknowledgement of one's *real* failings is good, the gratuitous eating of worms *not* put before us by God does not nourish our souls a bit."[6] As an occasional worm eater, I find the distinction she draws helpful.

God's Power to Save

Anyone who takes his or her faith seriously is bound to get discouraged at times. Some time ago I led a discussion on journaling as a spiritual discipline. When the discussion rolled around to the merits of reviewing journals, one young woman challenged the notion that such reviews are inevitably encouraging. In fact, she said, to see how little distance you have traveled over time can be downright discouraging. I agreed. My pilgrimage has been littered with high hopes for a holier life. Tested against the rigors of daily living, they have met with sputtering, thudding defeat.

A number of years ago I was feeling particularly discouraged. I seemed to be going nowhere. As far as I could tell it was not for lack of trying. I was working hard at spiritual disciplines, reading all the right books, aspiring to higher heights, but all, apparently, for nothing. Old temptations were finding new ways to distract me. Resolutions to change, however intense, eventually proved anemic. In my journal I lamented about "the yawning gap between where I long to be and where I know I am now." Then I added, "Something in me finds it hard to imagine that God is not as frustrated and impatient with me as I am with myself."

A week later I received a stinging, though ultimately hopeful, rebuke. I was meditating on a text in Isaiah when a verse bowled me over. I had never experienced anything quite like it before, nor have I since. In this text the Lord is challenging Israel: "Do you think I lack the power to save?" (Is 50:2 REB). The words bolted off the page. I was given some sense of the majesty of the One who was speaking, to me, and it drove me face down to the ground. "Do you think I lack the power to save?" It gradually dawned on me that all my impatience, all my tempestuous striving for growth, all my paralyzing discouragement were not signs of genuine spiritual intensity. In unguarded moments I had taken pride in the fervor of my struggle. Underneath it all I was haughtily questioning God. I was telling him that he simply did not have the power to save me; apparently I was too tough a case for him to handle. As I was led to reflect on all that God had done in Christ to secure my salvation, the ludicrousness and offensiveness of my own discouragement became more and more clear. "Do you think I lack the power to save?" No, Lord, I know now. You have that power.

That experience changed my life. While I have had many moments of discouragement since then, invariably those words come back—"Do you think I lack the power to save?"—and I am freed from allowing those moments to become a prevailing disposition. The benefit of that meditation was twofold. First, I was invited into a new level of trust in God and his power to work out my salvation. Second, I saw my discouragement for what it really was—a subtle form of self-absorption. Since that encounter I have never taken myself so seriously again.

Deeply discouraged, a good friend of Underhill's wrote and listed her many failings. Underhill responded (the closeness of their friendship may explain her candor):

To the alarming list of innate vices which you have managed to get together I should like to add another: Pride. All this preoccupation with your own imperfection is not humility, but an insidious form of spiritual pride. What do you *expect* to be? A saint? . . . Never allow yourself to be pessimistic about your own state. Look outwards instead of inwards.[7]

That outward look is, of course, the faith-filled look to God and his power to save in spite of all appearances to the contrary when we look inwards. Perhaps Underhill was aware that she was echoing the thought of one of her favorite writers, John of the Cross. He characterized anger with ourselves as "unhumble impatience" and chided beginners in the faith for aspiring "to become saints in a day."[8] In the same letter Underhill exhorts her friend with words medicinal to any of us prone to discouraging self-analysis: "Try to see yourself less as a complex individual, and more as a quite ordinary scrap of the universe."[9] Stripped from their context, her advice could well sound belittling, but Underhill is inviting her friend to see that her conversion rests not on the puny willpower of a scrap of the universe but ultimately on the will of this universe's Creator. That is profoundly hopeful. It is also an invitation to trust.

The Paradoxes of Spiritual Growth

To trust in God's grace means being suspicious of our own ability to evaluate our spiritual state. The Spirit's work in a human heart is anything but predictable or quantifiable. My ways are not your ways, says the Lord. Nowhere is this more true than in his work in our inner lives. Jonathan Edwards, that penetrating observer of spiritual experience, noted that God's work in his saints is often "exceeding mysterious and unsearchable," leaving them in a "confused chaos."[10] The wind blows where it blows. The trick is not to get distracted by appearances. If we have genuinely surrendered our souls to God, we can trust him with our soul's progress. Underhill cautions against putting too much credence in our own self-evaluative skills: "Please at once check the habit of getting the bulb out of the dark to see how it is getting on! It is impossible, and also undesirable for you to judge your own progress. Just go along simply, humbly, naturally, and when tempted to self-occupation of this or any other sort, make a quiet act of trust in God."[11]

If my ability to read my own spiritual barometer is risky at best, I should accept and embrace the mystery of spiritual growth with all its paradoxes and contraries. I should trust God with the state of my soul.

When our lives are grounded in a posture of trust, we achieve a healthy measure of distance from the inevitable highs and lows of Christian experience. It is not that we suspect all spiritual experiences, joyful or painful. But we learn to be discerning. Underhill pointed out that religious experiences had psychological and spiritual dimensions. While psychological feelings had their place, a wise Christian would focus on the spiritual dimension. How do we discern the difference between the two? Underhill offers helpful guidance: "The spiritual side is always deep, quiet, peaceful, humbling. All this you have and this is the valuable part and absolutely safe. Keep close to that and gently move away from the vivid, passionately rapturous type of reaction."[12] Underhill is not denying there is a place for rapture and ecstasy. The problem is that, especially for young believers, experiences are too easily sought as ends in themselves. Underhill offers this corrective to another correspondent: "Your conversion means giving yourself to God, not having nice religious feelings. Many of the Saints never had 'nice religious feelings'; but they did have a sturdy self-oblivious devotion to God alone."[13]

If religious excitement can distract us from the truer work of the Holy Spirit, spiritual dryness can do the same. Underhill wrote this sage piece of advice to a correspondent distracted by dryness:

> I think the upshot of it all is, that you are still far too much inclined to make feeling the test of religion. All that matters in religion is giving ourselves without reserve to God, and keeping our wills tending towards Him. This we can always do; but to feel devout, fervent, aware of His presence, etc., is beyond our control. Everyone goes through "dry" times. . . . All lies in how we take them—with patience, or with restlessness.[14]

How do we know if we are truly trusting God's grace through the agonies and ecstasies of spiritual growth? Underhill's comments give us a valuable clue. If our hearts are truly fixed on God, our inner restlessness will give way to his patience. If the outer test of true faith is charity to others, the inner test of true faith may well be patience with ourselves and God's work in us. Both are forms of that highest Christian virtue—self-forgetfulness.

Taking the Long View

Trusting God's grace means taking the long view of God's work in our lives. We may wish it were otherwise, but saints are not made in a day. I firmly believe that God is committed to our transformation, that he delights in a human soul making headway. I believe, with Kierkegaard, that the most wonderful evidence of God's power is not his creation of the cosmos from nothing, but the fact that he "creates saints . . . out of sinners."[15] But whatever our conception of how God effects change in our lives, there is no room for romantic naiveté. We can be guilty of what Underhill's mentor, Baron von Hügel, dubbed as the vice of too many a Christian—"tidying up reality."[16] Whatever transformation the gospel calls me to, I do not want to be guilty of tidying up reality. I am convinced that it is in the real world—the stop and start again, three steps forward, two steps back world—that God will do his work in my life.

His work will take time. But as we wait in hope (wait, in this sense, is another word for trust), we remember everything that God has done to secure our salvation. He has created this world, sent his Son, left his Spirit and incorporated us into his church. One day, he assures us, our salvation will be complete. Given the magnificent scope of God's work (as Julian of Norwich wrote, "the greatest deeds be already done"[17]), it does seem a rather small thing for God to ask us to trust him with the rest—the slow, painstaking but inevitable dawning of salvation in our small and stubborn hearts. Underhill counsels, "*Be* simple and dependent, acknowledge once for all the plain fact that you have nothing of your own, offer your life to God and trust Him with the ins and outs of your soul as well as everything else!"[18] Living in the disciplined serenity of a posture of trust, Underhill invites us to something far richer than the most spectacular and dramatic of spiritual highs: "Keep the deep steady permanent peace, in the long run [it is] more precious and more fruitful than the dazzling light."[19] Those who trust in God's grace take the long view. They have learned, with Underhill, that it is "the steady course, not the ecstasy, that counts in the end."[20]

Questions for Reflection and Discussion

1. How have you dealt with feelings of discouragement prompted by a lack of progress in your spiritual life?

2. Does the notion of prevenient grace ring true with your own experience?

Why or why not?

3. In what specific instances has God's prevenient grace operated in your life?

4. What is the fundamental difference between self-disgust and genuine humility?

5. What is the problem with trying to evaluate our own spiritual state?

6. In what particular places of discouragement in your life may God be calling you to take the long view, to trust more fully in his power to save?

THE OUTER JOURNEY

The gifts of Christian pilgrimage, even those gifts we first experience as obstacles, are not given to be hoarded. These gifts are given to be shared. Secure in following Jesus, undaunted by obstacles, we are freed to walk the outer journey. Aelred of Rievaulx, Margery Kempe, George Herbert and the Celtic saints are companions on this leg of the journey. They invite us to live out a full-orbed faith, rooted in a love for God that naturally spills out in service to neighbor and world.

NINE

CELEBRATING SPIRITUAL FRIENDSHIPS
Aelred of Rievaulx

How very good and pleasant it is
  when kindred live together in unity!

PSALM 133:1

*It is of God that we should be sustained amid the tribulations of our exile by
the advice and assistance of friends, until we come to God himself.*

RICHARD ROLLE (C. 1300-1349)

*Then I saw in my dream [Christian and Faithful] went very lovingly on
together, and had sweet discourse of all things that happened to them in their
pilgrimage: and thus Christian began: "My honoured and well beloved
brother Faithful, I am glad that I have overtaken you and that God has so
tempered our spirits that we can walk as companions in this so pleasant a
path."*

JOHN BUNYAN (1628-1688)

RAISED IN THE SCOTTISH COURT DURING THE TWELFTH CENTURY, AELRED
of Rievaulx (1109-1167) was a close childhood friend of King David I. From
his earliest days he loved to be with friends. As a school boy "the charm
of my companions pleased me very much, I gave my whole soul to affection
and devoted myself to love . . . so that nothing seemed to me more sweet,
nothing more agreeable, nothing more practical, than to love."[1] But such
natural affections ultimately needed schooling in the ways of Christ. As a
young courtier Aelred struggled with sexual sin. It was not until a profound

conversion and a decision to enter a monastic order at twenty-four that Aelred experienced the deepest of friendships.

A Friend to Many

Eventually Aelred became the leader, or abbot, of a burgeoning monastic community at Rievaulx. Yet this gifted scholar and shrewd administrator never allowed the demands of his work to deter him from exercising his greatest gift, a remarkable capacity for sharing love and friendship. One young man who entered the order, Simon, became a particularly close friend to Aelred. When Simon suddenly died, Aelred offered this heartfelt elegy for his dearest friend:

> Why have I tried to hide my feelings, and refused to talk about my sorrow? . . . Perhaps, by talking about Simon's death and weeping over him, my heart may rid itself of its burden. . . . He was my son in age, my father in example of holiness, my friend in godly love. . . . What do I care if streams of tears flow from my eyes throughout the day and night? Weep then, not because Simon has been taken up into heaven, but because Aelred has been left on earth, alone.[2]

As an abbot of a large community Aelred guided the spiritual life of the monks. He did so with great sensitivity. His *Pastoral Prayer* gives us a glimpse of the passionate gentleness of this man:

> For their sakes, Lord, if not for mine,
> teach him whom you have made to be their teacher,
> lead him whom you have bidden to lead them,
> rule him who is their ruler.
> Teach me, therefore, sweet Lord
> how to restrain the restless, comfort the discouraged,
> and support the weak.
> Teach me to suit myself to everyone
> according to his nature, character and disposition,
> according to his power of understanding or his lack of it,
> as time and place require, in each case,
> as you would have me do.
>
> . . . .
> For you, sweet Lord, know how much I love them,
> how I yearn over them, and how my heart goes out to them.[3]

Aelred spent the last ten years of his life racked in arthritic pain. At the end, he was unable to leave his cell. Walter Daniel, friend and biographer, recalls a lovely scene, typical of Aelred's last years:

> Every day [the brethren came to his cell] and sat in it, twenty or thirty at a time, to talk together of the spiritual delights of the Scriptures. . . . There was nobody to say to them, "Get out, go away, do not touch the Abbot's bed"; they walked and lay about his bed and talked with him as a little child prattles with his mother.[4]

Aelred was a remarkable man, the kind of person I would be honored to have as a spiritual guide or friend.

Thankfully, Aelred not only modeled spiritual friendship in his living, he also taught about it in his writing. Through penning his classic *On Spiritual Friendship* Aelred has become the teacher of many men and women.

The Nature and Source of Spiritual Friendships

A delightfully simple definition of spiritual friendship forms the opening line of his treatise: "Here we are, you and I, and I hope a third, Christ, is in our midst."[5] Immediately we warm to the voice of a wise friend who invites us to rethink the place of friendship in the life of faith. For Aelred the acknowledged presence of Christ was central to spiritual friendships.

Christ himself was the model friend. He extended his friendship to women and men such as Mary and Martha, and Peter, James and John. But more than that, only the presence of the indwelling Christ can transform one's character and affections, making that person capable of the high standards of fidelity and selflessness that mark the deepest friendships. What ultimately distinguishes a spiritual friendship from a natural friendship is the presence of Christ. He becomes the initiator, sustainer, the very end itself of a spiritual friendship. Aelred asks, "What more sublime can be said of friendship, what more true, what more profitable, than that it ought to, and is proved to, begin in Christ, continue in Christ, and be perfected in Christ?"[6] I am thankful that my life has been graced with a few such friendships. Whatever a friend and I may be doing together, be it serious or casual, somehow as friends we know that Christ is with us. I count such friendships among the very richest of life's gifts.

But where does spiritual friendship come from? What is its theological source? Aelred points to the principle of community evident everywhere in creation (even animals seem to delight in each other's company). A "certain love of companionship," he writes, is apparent.[7] The pervasiveness of this love of companionship in creation is hardly surprising, though, when we remember that the Creator himself is triune—Father, Son and Holy Spirit. He lives in companionship, an eternal friendship if you will, marked by mutual love, common vision, and intimate joy. God's capacity and desire for friendship leads Aelred to offer an inspired paraphrase of 1 John 4:16: "God is friendship . . . [and] he that abides in friendship, abides in God, and God in him."[8] Aelred challenges us to reimagine our spiritual friendships, to see them for what they are or can be—a participation in the very life of God himself. Little wonder then that when we taste spiritual friendship we feel we are tasting something of heaven.

The Medicine of Friends

When I met Dave that night, I was deeply troubled. I had been wrestling with an acute temptation for months, wrestling and losing in the grip of a force that left me powerless. Far too much of my mental and spiritual energy was being absorbed by this battle. I felt weary in the fight, discouraged, ashamed. I also felt that I had no one to talk to. Perhaps my friends would be embarrassed if I opened up my heart and shared the true nature of my struggles. Besides, I feared their rejection. I was feeling the weight of secrecy.

Dave and I chatted in the living room. It was a cold winter's night and every half hour or so I got up to stoke the fire and throw in a few more logs. Our conversation started in light, familiar territory, but I knew instinctively that the time was right to trust my friend with some of the deepest secrets of my heart. I fumbled through lengthy prefatory rambles. I shifted my body in my chair as if a new position might grant me the freedom to say what needed to be said. Eventually I got around to sharing what was really tearing at my heart.

Dave listened. He never flinched. He never downplayed the dark recklessness of my failings, but he never judged me or gave me even the slightest indication that he thought less of me because of my struggles. As he gave me space to talk, I felt increasing ease. The heaviness of shame and self-loathing lifted from my spirit. I felt new freedom. In sharing my struggles I had been loosed from the shackles of secrecy. With the release of long unspoken words it was as if I had broken their spell. The battle was not over, but what mercifully did end was my sense of powerlessness in the fight. When Dave left that night I felt like a new person. I could well affirm with Aelred that "the best medicine in life is a friend."[9]

Spiritual friends are those to whom Aelred says "we can fearlessly entrust our hearts and all its secrets."[10] But such friends are not only open to hear about the dark and troubled side of our lives. We also trust them deeply enough to share our bright victories. A spiritual friend, writes Aelred, is "one to whom you can unblushingly make known what progress you have made in the spiritual life."[11] Sometimes it is just as hard to talk about our achievements as it is our failures. We fear being misunderstood for sounding triumphalistic or smug. We want someone to trust the genuineness of the gratitude and pleasure we are feeling in our spiritual growth, even when we inevitably lapse into theological cliché in describing it. We want our friends to feel joy with us, not envy or suspicion.

The Guidance of Friends

Spiritual friends not only grant us the freedom to share the gains and setbacks we experience on our spiritual journey, they also help us chart the very course of that journey. Sometimes I am the least capable person of assessing my own spiritual progress (or regress). It is as if I have become overly familiar with myself, blind to some of my weaknesses, blind to some of my strengths. I overestimate imaginary achievements and I am totally oblivious to genuine gains. In short, I am like every human being, a muddle to myself. I need the thoughtful insights of others to truly get a bearing on the state of my soul. Spiritual friends are an enormous gift to us. The light of their insight can burn away banks of fog that otherwise leave us feeling stranded and disoriented.

I remember meeting Dave in front of the public library. It was a bright June day. I was at the end of a five-year contract in my ministry to university students, unclear about my future, unsure of whether my years in ministry had prepared me for the future, whether they pointed me in any hopeful direction. In my mid-thirties I was close enough to forty to be anxiously looking for signs of vocational achievement or at least vocational clarity. I was feeling high levels of uncertainty and insecurity.

Dave heard me out, but he was not about to second my confusion. He talked with sensitivity and conviction about what he saw happening in my life, chronicling fruit from my ministry, labeling gifts that were emerging. He affirmed the usefulness of what I was doing now and talked hopefully about the future. His words were a salve, not because of any superficial cheer they brought but because they were true words, words that only he could speak. Only he knew me so well, and only he had earned my full trust. They were healing words, reminding me that God was at work in my life. Our conversation was a strategic pointer, directing me further along the way of Christ in my life.

The Hard Disciplines of Spiritual Friendship

On these two occasions, and there have been many others, Dave has been a wonderful spiritual friend to me. I hope that I have been able to reciprocate that friendship. Aelred insists that the intimacy of spiritual friends must be characterized by mutuality. In what must have been a boldly egalitarian insight for his day, Aelred sees the principle of mutuality implicit in the creation story. He refers to the image of Eve coming from Adam's side and makes this striking comment: "How beautiful it is that the second human being was taken from the side of the first, so that nature might teach that human beings are equal and, as it were, collateral, and that there is in human affairs neither a superior nor an inferior, a characteristic of true friendship."[12] Incidentally, some of the greatest spiritual friendships have crossed gender lines: Monica and Augustine, Clare and Francis, Teresa of Ávila and John of the Cross. In that sense there has been something truly subversive about spiritual friendships. They have made equals of those society invariably wanted to slot into traditional hierarchies. The great church father Jerome wrote that "friendship either finds equals or makes them."[13]

On another occasion Dave was on the edge of a life shaping decision. Some were counseling him to go one way. I found myself counseling him to go in the other. When it became increasingly clear that he was about to choose what I could only see as a destructive option, I knew I needed to talk to him more frankly. I remember endlessly rehearsing the points I wanted to make, changing their order, trying to find that delicate balance of truth and grace. I did not relish the prospect of confrontation. Even the thought of it made my stomach churn.

One night after a game of pick-up hockey I drove Dave home and pulled into the curb to drop him off at his apartment. I knew I had to talk. I made my case as plainly as I could. It was hard, not so much because I hate confrontation but because I was calling my best friend's judgment into question and I risked hurting him deeply. Even though I assured him that I was committed to support him whatever he decided to do, I was haunted by the fear that our friendship might never fully recover.

Dave listened. He accepted my perspective with remarkable grace. We talked for a long time and eventually we prayed together. In the end Dave saw for himself where God was calling him at his moment of decision. Our gut-level conversation may have played some small role. Perhaps the wounds of a friend are indeed more tolerable than the kisses of an enemy. Hard as it was, our frank conversation knitted our souls together in new places. Aelred writes that "a man owes truth to his friend, without which the name of friendship has no value."[14] The disciplines of spiritual friendship are not always painless, but they are always constructive.

The Core of Spiritual Friendships

Some spiritual friendships grow naturally. My friendship with Dave grew out of planning summer camps together. At other times we may need to take more initiative. Perhaps an already existing friendship is ripe for a deeper experience of spiritual kinship. Such friends may come from a small group. Prayer partnerships are another natural place for spiritual friendships to flourish. Many have discovered that a relationship with a spiritual director can become a spiritual friendship. For five years I visited a director monthly. She was an older woman, rich in experience in the faith. I found her to be a tremendously affirming presence; like a spiritual mother she nurtured and guided my prayer life. I am forever in her debt, and as much as she has given to me, I know that our relationship has also been an encouragement to her.

Wherever you may find a spiritual friend, get together and share your pilgrimages—where you have been, where you are now. Talk about your prayer lives, their strengths and weaknesses. Share about particular spiritual disciplines that draw you closer to God. Give to each other the two gifts Aelred notes that spiritual friends can give, gifts that are free but inexpressibly powerful. One, live a life of authenticity and integrity before

God. It will, among other things, leave a deep and wholesome impression on your friend. As I think about the legacy of Dave's friendship in my life, it is his very living that has been his greatest gift to me. It inspired me when I first began to know him fifteen years ago, and it continues to inspire me. Two, pray for your friend. Pray for his or her growth in the faith as intensely as you would pray for your own. Make a habit of praying together. You may even choose to confess your sins to one another or hold each other accountable in the area of spiritual disciplines.

Just as I finished the first draft of this chapter, I received a phone call from Dave. (He now lives half a continent away.) We caught up on each other's news and then had the opportunity to reflect back on the history of our friendship. He had no idea I had been writing about spiritual friendship, but he noted that our friendship began when we recognized in each other a passion for God. Since that time, he said, we have been given ways to help each other stay true to that passion. I think he is right. Our friendship has been about a lot of things—working together in youth ministry, coediting a college newspaper, sharing vacations, bemoaning the fates of our favorite hockey teams, cohosting a radio show, delighting in each other's children—the list goes on. Our friendship has been rich and varied. But at its core, in grace, there has been a mutual passion for God and a desire to help each other keep the flame of our first love burning. It is long, hard work. We were never meant to do it alone.

As much as you will want to stay true to the core of spiritual friendships, you will also want to avoid the temptation of becoming too narrowly "spiritual." Talk together about all of life, the big, the small, the significant and the mundane. Together you will stretch your sense of what is spiritual until it embraces all of life. There will be time to help clarify each other's thinking, time to confront and time to console. There will be a time for talking and a time for listening. There will be a time for laughing and a time for sighing. There will be you, there will be your friend, and the presence of a third in your midst.

Questions for Reflection and Discussion

1. According to Aelred, what makes a spiritual friendship different from a natural friendship?

2. What experience have you had with spiritual friendship?

3. What are the valuable gifts such friends have given you?

4. What have you been able to give them in return?

5. What experiences have you had of the "hard disciplines" of spiritual friendship?

6. What steps do you need to take to develop or enhance spiritual friendships in your life?

TEN

LOVING THE UNLOVABLE
Margery Kempe

Let Israel be glad in its Maker;
  let the children of Zion rejoice in their King.
Let them praise his name with dancing,
  making melody to him with tambourine and lyre.

PSALM 149:2-3

God the Creator arranged things so that we need each other.

BASIL OF CAESAREA (C. 330-379)

The serious Christian, set down for the first time in a Christian community, is
likely to bring with him a very definite idea of what Christian life together
should be and to try to realize it. But God's grace speedily shatters such
dreams. Just as surely as God desires to lead us to a knowledge of genuine
Christian fellowship, so surely must we be overwhelmed by a great
disillusionment with others, with Christians in general, and, if we are
fortunate, with ourselves.

DIETRICH BONHOEFFER (1906-1945)

M Y DAUGHTER CAME THROUGH THE DOOR, BARELY ABLE TO HOLD BACK HER
disbelief. She had been to a youth group meeting and watched a video
where a speaker railed against all manner of worldly vices, dancing among
them. In the first flush of seventh-grade dances my daughter could not
contain her incredulity. "Dancing? What could be wrong with dancing?"

I must confess that I took some delight in her response. During my own
teen years dancing was one of the great evils that threatened to take the

Christian teen down the slippery slope of perdition. It may have looked like fun, and certainly resonated with those restless hormones raging through my body, but Satan often appeared as an angel of light. The angel/demon of dancing! Christian teenager, beware. I timidly, and somewhat resentfully, stayed away.

There was, of course, some wisdom in the warning. Modern dancing at its outer limits can be provocatively sensual, even dangerously violent. But that had not been my daughter's experience and I took pleasure in her sense of security in negotiating what is admittedly a gray area in a world that is, after all, littered with gray areas. What she had not fallen prey to was the spirit of legalism that locates evil in a few select activities—smoking, drinking and dancing for example—and then takes pride in avoiding them, all the while ignoring subtler but no less pernicious expressions of evil in soap operas or too frequent trips to the shopping mall. She had resisted the oversimplified world of legalism. Perhaps she knew that it is the dance of charity—creative love of God and neighbor—that must be the heartbeat of her faith.

Redemptive Images of Dancing

I will never forget a dance held during a summer teen camp I directed on Prince Edward Island. About forty teenagers and camp staff squeezed into a lovely century-old community hall. There local musicians and dancers taught us the basics of contredance, a Scottish folk dance that bears a rough resemblance to square dancing. As you might imagine, the teenagers were skeptical at first. Eventually, though, the music of the guitar and fiddle proved infectious. All of us danced—arm in arm, twirling, singing, stepping, bowing. Sweat dripped off our foreheads, but the dance went on. As the air grew heavier and hotter and as the dances grew faster, we could feel an almost palpable sense of joy descend on us. Gradually all of us—staff and campers, sophisticated urban kids and work-booted kids from the farm, the jovial and confident, the reticent and the insecure—shed our differences and were drawn into a sweet sense of oneness.

When the dance finally ended, we walked out of the hall into the cool of a beautiful summer evening. One of our local instructors, a veteran of countless contredances, said it was simply the best dance he had ever experienced. There was indeed something magical about that night. It was one of the most wholesomely pleasurable experiences of my life.

Of course, the Scriptures are not without images of dancing. Miriam dances before the Lord at the crossing of the Red Sea, and a whole nation of women joins her. The psalmists more than once exhort us to dance. David danced with wild abandon before the Lord when the ark of the covenant was restored to Israel. While his dance aroused consternation in the heart of his wife Michal, we are left with little doubt that it brought joy to God's heart.

For another redemptive image of dancing we need look no further than a fascinating book by Margery Kempe (c. 1373-d. after 1433), a laywoman who left behind a remarkable chronicle of her life and religious experiences, titled simply *The Book of Margery Kempe.* Margery lived out her faith with great intensity. She achieved a deep sense of intimacy with Jesus; little wonder that when she receives a vision of the life to come it centers on an arresting image of communion with Jesus. Entering heaven she hears Jesus speak to her with words of deep affection:

> Thou art to Me a singular love, daughter, and therefore I promise thee thou shalt have a singular grace in Heaven . . . for with Mine own hands which were nailed to the Cross, I will take thy soul from thy body with great mirth and melody, with sweet smells and good odours, and offer it to My Father in Heaven. I shall take thee by the one hand . . . and so shalt thou dance in Heaven . . . for I may call thee dearly bought, and Mine own dearworthy darling.[1]

Heaven, in this striking image, is a place where we dance with Jesus. Come through the gates, see his welcoming face, take his beckoning hand, and feel yourself swept into a dance of unspeakable joy and rapture. Dance with Jesus, the Lord of the Dance.

It is an entrancing image of our destiny. Eventually we will all dance with Jesus. But if such an image anticipates our future, it is also deeply suggestive for our present. If dancing with Jesus is our future, time to cultivate that partnership in the present must be a top priority. After all, great partnerships in dance are the product of arduous hours of sweat and strain and practice. Gradually a deep familiarity develops; each partner comes to intuitively sense the other's presence, and the end result, in all its apparent effortlessness, is stirring and beautiful. Striving for that kind of familiarity in our relationship with Jesus now is the best way to prepare ourselves for the celestial dance floor that awaits us

Embracing the Unlovable

But dancing is a metaphor that not only highlights our destiny and challenges us to develop intimacy with Jesus. Jesus' dance with Margery also has profound social implications. Give the metaphor full play in our imaginations and it has the potential to revolutionize relationships within our Christian communities.

Margery Kempe was a very devout woman. The relentless spiritual desire that characterizes her life cannot help but be chastening to our own relative complacency. Margery seemed oblivious to the soft standards of "church culture" that, in our own day as well, can rob the spiritual life of its vigor. Some might say Margery Kempe was a saint. Maybe she was. Some of her contemporaries held her in high regard. But that is not the whole story of Margery Kempe, for while some revered her, others, some of them devout Christians, thought she was dangerous, even mad. Her years of uncontrollable weeping over the passion of Jesus impressed some but alienated others. She was arrested by church authorities on a number of occasions, severely questioned and rebuked. Even in our own century the legacy of her witness is hotly debated. Martin Thorton, a highly regarded authority on English spirituality, holds Margery's prayer life up as a model to which we should all aspire.[2] On the other hand, Charles Williams, a deeply spiritual man (and no stranger to spiritual eccentricity himself), dismisses Margery as "a general nuisance."[3]

As a reader of *The Book of Margery Kempe* I have been pulled in both directions. I have admired the sheer passion of her faith and her indifference to standards of social conformity in her pursuit of godliness. Her visions of encounters with Jesus can be deeply moving. Invariably they ring true to the spirit of the Jesus of the gospels. At other times, though, I have found myself exasperated. Margery's endless displays of unrestrained weeping seem excessive. Perhaps she battled a form of mental illness. She is obsessed with her own spiritual experience and its public justification by appropriate church authorities. It seems far too easy for her to wish God's judgment on those who questioned her legitimacy. In short, meeting Margery Kempe, even in her *Book*, can be highly exasperating. At times I felt much more like shunning her than dancing with her.

But there is Jesus, dancing with Margery. He knows Margery as she truly is and welcomes her home. He holds her firmly and joyfully, and he dances with mirth and melody. He looks into her eyes, red with weeping, and calls her "dearly bought, mine own dear worthy darling." Jesus wants to dance with Margery. The arms that reach out to her once stretched across a rough wooden beam. He died for her so that he could dance with her.

A Subversive Dance

This clearly is no ordinary dance. Traditional dances often confirm and solidify a certain social order. In George Eliot's *Silas Marner* the small village of Raveloe is galvanized by the most important dance of the year. As always the host is Squire Cass, the most prominent man of the village (even if he is ludicrously self-absorbed). Local fiddler Solomon Macey has been hired to provide music. With the opening notes of the familiar tune "Sir Roger de Coverly," the crowd knows it is time to dance and, as it should, the dance begins with Squire Cass taking the arm of Mrs. Crackenthorpe. The rector and Mrs. Osgood follow them onto the dance floor and, guided by these time-honored cues, the people of Raveloe pair off in ways that appropriately mirror their social standing in the village. The dance is a huge success. All are happy to play their respective roles. The harmony achieved in the dance is a reflection of everyone's willingness to assume his or her proper place in the pecking order of a small Victorian English village. The dance confirms and celebrates that order. Eliot writes, "That was as it should be—that was what everybody had been used to—and the charter of Raveloe seemed to be renewed by the ceremony."[4]

Jesus' dance with Margery is different. Here the risen Christ, the enthroned Son, takes the despised Margery and sweeps her into the very center of the dance. Far from confirming and celebrating human constructs of social order, this dance celebrates a riotous upheaval of every notion of social propriety and convention, defying and undermining old orders even as it brashly creates a new order. Human pecking orders will not confer identity in this new order. Jesus knows too well all the injustices and insecurities they breed.

As each of us dances with Jesus we are simultaneously humbled and ennobled—humbled because regardless of what level of social status we have achieved, whether through talent, wealth or education, we each realize that we are simply unworthy of the attention of the divine Son, but we are also ennobled by receiving a new identity, each being individually affirmed and cherished. Sweeping across the center of the dance floor, faces are marked forever by the loving gaze of Jesus.

I believe that if we begin to let this metaphor loose in our imaginations it will revolutionize our relationships. In the new order of Jesus there is little room for romantic conceptions of human community. Creating genuine Christian community is never easy. There are people in our lives who like Margery Kempe get under our skin. They make the new order hard to achieve. Subtly or not so subtly we place such people in categories of the undesirable, the unworthy. We keep them at a distance. Consciously or unconsciously we write them off as being beneath us, uninteresting, or simply too bothersome to bring into our circle of genuine community. Jesus' dance with Margery forces us to see our own encounters with the irritating and the unlovable as invitations to live in the reality of his new order, a kingdom where we have all been made one, both humbled and ennobled by the loving gaze of Jesus. Without this exercising of our imaginations —some call it faith—we will remain mired in the pettiness of our own prejudices and will lack the fierce resolve it takes to build genuine community.

The Prickly Disciplines of Community

At one point in Frederick Buechner's novel *Brendan,* the story of a sixth-century Celtic saint, the title character sets sail on a long voyage of penance. Brendan's pride and explosive anger have precipitated the tragic death of a young priest under his care. Solitude on the seas will give him time and space to search his soul. Strangely enough, Brendan decides to take the unlikely Malo with him. Malo is a bitter, foul-spirited monk. True to form, he needles Brendan at every opportunity. He gleefully throws Brendan's folly and sin into his face, and rubs salt into his open wounds. In spite of this blatant cruelty, eventually Brendan chooses to confess his sins regularly to the repulsive Malo.

Brendan's choice of traveling companions likely strikes us as excessively masochistic, but it is not that simple. Brendan knows that as much as Malo irritates and vexes him, Malo is also his salvation. Pride has led Brendan to his downfall. The merciless barbs of Malo are a healing salve, inviting Brendan to cultivate the spirit of humility he so desperately craves.

So often it is the very people who irritate us and vex us the most who have the most to teach us. The reserved academic finds her interaction with a social activist in her church to be positively wearying. She finds herself shunning the activist at every opportunity. The activist's opinions are always so cut and dried, leaving no room for subtlety. But it could be that this activist is being used by God to challenge and even correct the cautious passivity of the academic. Her complex abstractions are often self-protective measures that excuse her from putting herself on the line in working for social justice.

Or take the perfectionist. He is horrified by the new member on his church board. While this new member's people skills are strong (he exudes relational warmth), he also seems incapable of remembering on what day the board meets. This newcomer is the clear enemy to the perfectionist's hopes for a board that will run like clockwork. But viewed in another light the newcomer is a healthy irritant, challenging the perfectionist to balance his administrative precision with a genuine heart for people.

It is an unavoidable dynamic of genuine Christian community—the people who irritate us the most have the most to teach us. God places them in our path for a definite reason. Unfortunately, our instinctive response is to avoid an irritant's company at all costs. Some of us live forever on the fringes of genuine community because we are afraid of the sharp give and take of the inner workings of a local church. We seem to forget that a local church will be just as resolutely human and sinful as we ourselves. In fact this mutual chipping away at each other can be powerfully medicinal. Who are the healthy irritants in our lives? What does God want us to learn from them? Are we willing to submit to the sometimes prickly disciplines of Christian community? Are we willing to dance with the Margery Kempes of our lives?

These people who get under our skin often warm the same pews we do. There is the spoiled child determined to make a farce out of children's story time every Sunday morning, the insolent teenager scowling through joyous hymns, the small group member talking incessantly, oblivious to the thoughts of others. We all know these people. How would it revolutionize our perception of these, our fellow believers, if we could see

Jesus dancing with them? The deacon with the heart of gold but a sharp, fierce tongue as well, the minister who evaporates our spirits with sermons full of lazy observations and overused illustrations—both of them dancing with Jesus. The cantankerous, the stubborn, the dull, the meddlesome, the critical, the small-minded—each of them and each of us wounded, flawed and sinful in our own incorrigible ways. You and me—dancing with Jesus!

Questions for Reflection and Discussion

1. Reread Margery's vision of Jesus inviting her to dance. Imagine Jesus is making the same invitation to you. Do you feel worthy or unworthy, relaxed or awkward?

2. What might this exercise suggest about your relationship with Jesus?

3. What are you doing, or what might you do, that would help you develop familiarity with Jesus now?

4. Think of a "Margery" in your life. Imagine Jesus dancing with that person. What difference would it make if you were to see your fellow saints as Jesus sees them?

5. In what ways might God be wanting to use "irritating saints" to correct or challenge you?

6. What concrete commitments can you make that will help you submit to the prickly disciplines of Christian community?

ELEVEN

INSPIRING OTHERS TO GODLINESS
George Herbert

O Lord, who may abide in your tent?
  Who may dwell on your holy hill?
Those who walk blamelessly, and do what is right,
  and speak the truth from their heart.

PSALM 15:1-2

For God has [in the gospel] made no promises of mercy to the slothful and negligent. His mercy is only offered to our frail and imperfect, but best endeavours, to practise all manner of righteousness.

WILLIAM LAW (1686-1761)

[A person of character] will acquire the power to excite and arouse, a propulsive power. . . Only in character do I actually have the right to talk about what Christianity is; to confer (cordially!) with others about it in easy jargon is an assault upon Christianity, a lack of respect.

SØREN KIERKEGAARD (1813-1855)

I AM FORTUNATE TO LIVE IN A STATELY VICTORIAN HOME. ONE OF ITS STRIKING features is a spacious living room. Once two rooms, this room at one point in its history had a wall torn down. Now the room is nearly thirty feet long. Bookcases that line the full length of one wall add warmth, and at the far end of the room is a fireplace with an elegant mantelpiece. It is a lovely room, and it never looks better than when it is full of people.

My wife and I once hosted a party to say goodbye to friends who were leaving town. It was a grand evening. After food and drink a friend read a poem he had written in their honor. Another recited Shakespeare. Others brought out musical instruments and entertained. Even those who couldn't play an instrument tried. It may not have been music, but it was joyful noise. Laughter filled the room.

After everyone left I turned out the lights. I sat in the quietness of our living room, drinking up echoes of the music, conversation and laughter that still hung in the air. What a privilege to be able to welcome people into my home.

I also reflected about how these ways of hospitality had come to me through my parents. From as early as I can remember, my own home was full of guests—extended family, neighbors, visiting preachers and newcomers to our church. My parents' exercise of hospitality went well beyond the norm. During the period of the Vietnamese boat people, my parents built new rooms in their home and invited a Vietnamese family to live with us. Later they opened their home to a young woman dying of cancer. She spent the last weeks of her life there.

My parents have influenced me in countless ways. I recall receiving many words of correction and encouragement from both of them. Those words have been important. My father in particular has a gift with words. I have often sat under his teaching and learned a great deal. But ultimately, it is the ways of my parents that have left the deepest impression on me. Their very living, with open heart and open home, has marked my life with a power that words alone could never match.

Some people's lives, including people from the past, inspire us. On the wall of my study is a framed picture of George Herbert (1593-1633). He is certainly one of my heroes of the faith. I first encountered Herbert as an undergraduate English student required to study his poetry. Through the years I have returned to his work many times and have come to know more of his life. I have been drawn to the intense and yet quiet beauty of his spirit.

George Herbert was born into a distinguished English family from near the Welsh border. Although he was born into privileged circumstances his early life also had its trials. Before he reached the age of four, his father Richard died, leaving his mother to raise a large family on her own. By all accounts Lady Magdalene Herbert was a remarkable woman. She possessed a lively mind and a vigorous faith. She had a gift for hospitality and a heart of compassion for the poor. Magdalene Herbert was keenly aware of the influence her many guests would have on her children. Izaak Walton, Herbert's first biographer, tells us she was fond of saying "that as our bodies take a nourishment suitable to the meat on which we feed; so our souls do as insensibly take in vice by the example or conversation with wicked company."[1] If wicked company could unconsciously lead a child to vice, good company could subtly but powerfully train a child in virtue. It was a lesson not to be lost on George Herbert. The power of a godly life to stir others to holiness became one of the guiding principles of his life.

Herbert's Well-Tuned Life

Herbert's early life was marked by signs of great promise. He was a brilliant student, earning high academic awards. In his mid-twenties he was appointed orator of Cambridge University. It was a prestigious post. His immediate predecessors had vaulted from Cambridge to high positions in the royal court. The learning and wit Herbert displayed as orator drew the attention of King James. Herbert also sat as a member of Parliament. A career in the royal court seemed open to him.

But the lure of the court gave way to a deeper call in Herbert's heart. From the outset of his university studies he had been preparing for ordination in the Church of England. Ultimately Herbert was convinced that his greatest service to God and his country could be exercised in a life of pastoral service. Sickness and financial uncertainties delayed Herbert's plans for ordination, but in 1630 he and his wife Jane moved to the rural parish of Bemerton. Others viewed his retreat from the influential worlds of scholarship and politics as a crushing setback. For Herbert, his three years as an obscure country parson were the culmination of his life's work.

Herbert's goal as a parson was clear. Walton tells us that the night before his induction at St. Andrew's Church in Bemerton, he revealed to his friend Arthur Woodnoth what we might call today his mission statement: "Above all, I will be sure to live well, because the virtuous life of a clergyman is the most powerful eloquence to persuade all that see it to reverence and love, and at least to desire to live like him." Living virtuously was a parson's greatest opportunity to lead others into a life of holiness. As a master of rhetoric, a gifted orator and a brilliant poet, George Herbert knew all about the power of words. But he also knew their limitations. In the end a life of holiness was most eloquent. As he went on to explain to Woodnoth, "I know we live in an age that hath more need of good examples than precepts."[2] Perhaps this is true of every age, including our own.

Judging from the unanimous witness of his contemporaries, George Herbert lived that exemplary life. Exercising spiritual leadership in a parish made up mostly of uneducated country folk, he devoted himself to leading public worship, offering spiritual counsel to his parishioners and caring for the poor. Early in his ministry at Bemerton Herbert was visited by an old woman who lived in poverty. She intended to speak to him, but after she sputtered out a few words she became flustered and disoriented, no doubt intimidated by the reputation of the new parson. She was simply unable to speak. Herbert graciously took her hand, sat her down and put her at ease. He assured her that he wanted to listen to her, and after intently hearing her out he consoled her with words of spiritual encouragement and gave her money to ease her circumstances. She parted with new joy in her heart. Walton concludes the story, "Thus lowly, was Mr. George Herbert in his own eyes, and thus lovely in the eyes of others."[3]

George Herbert loved music. He claimed it "elevated his soul, and was his heaven upon earth."[4] During his years at Bemerton, twice a week, as long as his health permitted, he walked to nearby Salisbury Cathedral to sing and play music. On one of his walks he met a poor man with an overburdened horse. The horse's load had fallen onto the road. Both needed help, so Herbert took off his coat, helped the man and sent him off with a word of blessing. Herbert arrived late at the cathedral and his musical friends were shocked to see the usually impeccably neat parson dirty and disheveled. After listening to Herbert tell the story of the poor man, one of the musicians scolded Herbert for lowering himself to such demeaning work. Herbert replied that if he had not helped the man he would feel the sting of his own conscience. He had prayed for those in distress; he could hardly fail, then, to practice what he had prayed for. Furthermore, the memory of what he had done would "prove music to him at midnight," allowing him to sleep in peace. He concluded, "I praise God for this occasion," and then, as if enough attention had already been drawn to his act of charity, "And now let's tune our instruments."[5]

George Herbert indeed lived a well-tuned life, and these two incidents give us glimpses into the winsome character of his ministry at Bemerton. It was service marked by humility, ceaseless devotion to public and private prayer, and generous acts of compassion for the poor. Izaak Walton summarizes Herbert's witness: "Thus he lived, and thus he died, like a saint, unspotted of the world, full of alms-deeds, full of humility, and all the examples of a virtuous life."[6] While Walton's portrait of Herbert may be somewhat idealized, there is no reason to doubt his overall assessment. Nicholas Ferrar, one of Herbert's closest friends, a man of great devotion himself, testified that Herbert's life made him "justly a companion to the primitive Saints, and a pattern or more for the age he lived in."[7] Herbert's oldest brother, Edward, offered this tribute: "His life was most holy and exemplary, in so much that about Salisbury where he lived beneficed for many years, he was little less than sainted."[8] George Herbert sought to live a life that in all its particulars would inspire others to godliness. The desire of his heart had been granted.

Holiness in the Details

Although some may believe that the life of a seventeenth-century English parson seems too far removed from our own to offer any instruction, I don't agree. If anything, Herbert's conception of a life of virtue as one designed to teach and inspire others has particular relevance in our own day. Four hundred years after Herbert's birth we live in a world characterized by an aggressive form of individualism. Self is the ultimate authority. Whatever fulfills the self is pursued with unrestrained vigor. Thoughts of how other people are affected by our actions are clearly secondary thoughts. As long as our actions do not directly hurt or violate others, others have no right to question us. George Herbert turns this distorted view of life on its head. Rather than being content with a life that merely avoids flagrantly hurting others, he challenges us to see every moment of our lives for what it truly is—an opportunity charged with the potential to profoundly influence others for good. Herbert's vision is a sharp rebuttal to the spirit of our age.

Herbert's vision also challenges us to think about our own lives. George Herbert spent the last years of his life in a rural English parish. We all have our own parishes, communities where our lives have a profound impact on others. Herbert's witness challenges us to identify our parishes. For some of us our immediate family is our primary parish. For others it may be a close circle of friends, a small group, a network of relationships in our workplace or our neighborhood. Many of us could identify a number of parishes. With Herbert we need to think through how the very living of our lives is constantly marking, for good or ill, those people God has placed within our circle of influence.

Recently I spent some time establishing goals, praying and reflecting about what I could do that would truly make a difference in the year ahead. One of my resolutions was very simple and practical. I would spend the first hour of my day, from seven to eight in the morning, being available to my wife and children as they scurried through preparations for school. That hour can be a tense time. Early morning testiness and anxiety about the day ahead make for a strained atmosphere. As I prayed I was called to pay more attention to my conduct and disposition during that hour. Helpful acts and a calm spirit could make a huge difference, setting a tone for my family's day.

My success so far has been measured. But I remain committed to my resolution. So much of life has to do with careful attention to the routine and ordinary. A holy life that pleases God and inspires others is not built on grand sweeping gestures, but on disciplined attention to the small stuff of daily living. This understanding of a holy life informs Herbert's *The Country Parson*. In this treatise Herbert charmingly and precisely details how a parson's example must extend into every corner of his life. As to his family life, "the Parson is very exact in the governing of his house, making it a copy and model for his Parish."[9] Holiness was to be embodied in even the most ordinary details, from the choice of certain herbs over others for medicinal purposes to decisions about which parishioners would be invited to his home. The fabric of his life was to be genuinely and compellingly didactic. It was to be a seamless sermon to his parishioners.

The Didactic Life

In *The Country Parson* Herbert unravels the implications of "the didactic life," a life that would teach and instruct others in godliness. Of course a parson could teach parishioners through preaching and catechizing. Preaching could inflame listeners, inspiring them to godliness. Catechizing offered a unique opportunity to systematically teach parishioners. Herbert cherished both tasks but insisted they received power to move people only in the context of a holy life: "neither will they believe him in the pulpit, whom they cannot trust in his Conversation."[10] (By "conversation," Herbert means way of living). In fact holy living would be the most persuasive form of preaching. When parishioners needed correction, the parson had two vital sources of influence, a strong devotional life and an uncontentious spirit, "two great lights to dazzle the eyes of the misled."[11] Similarly, when a parson was criticized his best defense was not verbal: "Where contempt is, there is no room for instruction." Instead, the parson endeavored to win his parishioner's favor by "his holy and unblameable life . . . a courteous carriage, and winning behaviour."[12] When disputes arose between parishioners, the parson encouraged the estranged neighbors to share a meal together, adding "there is much preaching in this friendliness."[13]

I suppose that in attempting to live the didactic life we might be tempted to allow our lives to take on the air of a well-rehearsed theatrical performance. We may self-consciously do the right thing to put forward the best public face. Our faith could well collapse into a shallow moralism. Every good deed, every incident in our lives, could become a soapbox from which we could triumphantly proclaim the moral of the story to others. I have met such Christians, and frankly it is hard to imagine anything less attractive. Herbert's didactic life is not a life of heavy-handed moralism. It is rather a life so full of integrity and joy that it delights others and moves them toward imitation.

A Fully Human Life

George Herbert's commitment to live the didactic life also never tempted him to hide his own flawed humanity. It is true that his poetry is full of moments of joy and repose, as in the closing stanza of "The Call":

> Come, my Joy, my Love, my Heart:
> Such a Joy, as none can move:
> Such a Love, as none can part:
> Such a Heart, as joys in love.

But all was not stillness and light in Herbert's Christian experience. On his deathbed he sent his poems to Nicholas Ferrar, telling him, "[You] shall find in it a picture of the many spiritual conflicts that have passed betwixt

God and my soul."[14] It is an apt description of what we find in *The Temple,* published shortly after his death—poems that searchingly unveil deep-rooted struggles. If we were left with only the outline of Herbert's exemplary life, his achievement may well intimidate us. But in the poems of *The Temple* we see the fullness of his humanity, the complexities and contradictions so much a part of his life of faith.

George Herbert battled illness his entire adult life. Eventually he died of consumption at thirty-nine. In the grip of illness Herbert felt he was physically and spiritually suffocating. Yet God seemed indifferent. In "Home" he gives vent to his frustration:

> Come, Lord, my head doth burn, my heart is sick,
> While thou dost ever, ever stay:
> Thy long deferrings wound me to the quick,
> My spirit gaspeth night and day.
> Oh show thyself to me,
> Or take me up to thee!

For years Herbert wrestled with the exact nature of God's call. Was he called to the court or to the church? He longed for clarity but for years found none, as he confesses in these lines from "The Cross":

> Ah my dear Father, ease my smart!
> These contrarieties crush me: these cross actions
> Do wind a rope about, and cut my heart.

George Herbert remained single until his mid-thirties. Frequent references to "passion" and "lust" in *The Temple* suggest he experienced the fierce assaults of sexual temptation. In "The Pearl" he cries out to God, "My stuff is flesh, not brass." In "The Sinner" he confesses that in spite of all his aspirations to godliness, a search of his own heart reveals "quarries of pil'd vanities, / But shreds of holiness." There were times when Herbert chafed under the apparent harshness of God's ways, as he reveals in the opening stanza from "Discipline":

> Throw away thy rod,
> Throw away thy wrath:
> Oh my God,
> Take the gentle path.

In "The Search" Herbert admits to experiencing the absence of the God his soul craved:

> Whither, Oh whither art thou fled,
> My Lord, my Love?
> My searches are my daily bread;
> Yet never prove.
>
> My knees pierce th' earth, mine eyes the sky;
> And yet the sphere
> And center both to me deny
> That thou art there.

In all his experiences of weakness and brokenness, however, Herbert believed that God would ultimately bring healing to his soul. He articulates this belief in the following lines from "Repentance":

> But thou wilt sin and grief destroy;
> That so the broken bones may joy,
> And tune together in a well-set song,
> Full of his praises,
> Who dead men raises.
> Fractures well cur'd make us more strong.

George Herbert told the truth in his poetry. If the poems of *The Temple* often end on a note of resolution, it is a genuine, hard-earned resolution.

A Clear Yet Fragile Witness

How did Herbert reconcile his desire to live the exemplary, didactic life with the many spiritual conflicts that passed betwixt God and his soul? In the end, I think he chose to live in the tension of a fruitful paradox. He believed that as long as he genuinely aspired to the virtuous life, his own weakness, in the mystery of grace, could become the very place where God's strength would be revealed. The witness of his life was like that of stained glass windows in the churches he loved. On the one hand, as he confesses in "Windows," even in the loftiest tasks of his calling he was every bit as fragile as glass:

> Lord, how can man preach thy eternal word?
> He is a brittle crazy glass.

Still he remained a window through which God's grace could shine:

> Yet in thy temple thou dost him afford
> This glorious and transcendent place,
> To be a window through thy grace.

The mystery of God's strength being revealed in his weakness was, however, no excuse for laxness. The parson's words in preaching were not enough. They may pierce the ears but never the heart. Only in words and works combined could the didactic life in all its humanness be truly lived:

> Doctrine and life, colors and light, in one
> When they combine and mingle, bring
> A strong regard and awe: but speech alone
> Doth vanish like a flaring thing,
> And in the ear, not conscience ring.

I hope this sketch of Herbert's life and writing has begun to inspire you in the way Herbert has inspired me. Basking in the light of his witness I cannot help but examine my own life. I think of my own parishes—my family, friends, small group, neighbors, church community and town. I long to be a Christian whose way of living draws others to a fuller faith. Herbert's conception of the didactic life is compelling. Even more inspiring is his life, its artful blend of truth and beauty. But, like Herbert, I am not remotely interested in the pretense of godliness—the pasted-on smile, the easy religious jargon that sustains a soft faith. No, I hope in grace to live and speak truthfully, even when it means living with contradiction, being painfully but joyfully stretched on the cross of my own weakness and God's strength.

Do all our contradictions and weaknesses blight our efforts to live the didactic life? The witness of George Herbert's life assures us they do not. I think too of the godly men and women who have profoundly influenced my life. I am so grateful for the healing ways their lives have rubbed off on mine. But I have known these people well enough to know their weaknesses. Their stuff too is flesh, not brass. Weak and fragile? Yes, and yet the light shines through so clearly. We have all been given "this glorious and transcendent place, / To be a window through thy grace."

Questions for Reflection and Discussion

1. What impresses you about the life and witness of George Herbert?

2. Think of one person who inspired you in your Christian life. What was it about him or her that inspired you?

3. In what specific areas of your life would disciplined attention to the small stuff of daily living make your life more holy?

4. What are your parishes, or circles of influence?

5. Which parishes are in need of special attention at this time?

6. How do you deal with the tension of attempting to live an exemplary life for others while being honest about your flaws and contradictions?

TWELVE

CARING FOR CREATION
The Celtic Saints

O Lord, how manifold are your works!
In wisdom you have made them all;
the earth is full of your creatures.
Yonder is the sea, great and wide,
creeping things innumerable are there,
living things both small and great.

PSALM 104:24-25

What is a charitable heart? It is a heart which is burning with love for the
whole creation, for men, for the birds, for the beasts, for the demons—for all
creatures. He who has such a heart cannot see or call to mind a creature
without his eyes being filled with tears by reason of the immense compassion
which seizes his heart; a heart which is softened and can no longer bear to
see or learn from others of any suffering, even the smallest pain, being
inflicted upon a creature. . . . [Such a person will be] moved by the infinite
pity which reigns in the hearts of those who are becoming united with God.

ISAAC THE SYRIAN
(LATE SEVENTH CENTURY)

You never enjoy the world aright, till the Sea itself floweth in your veins, till
you are clothed with the heavens, and crowned with the stars. . . . Till you
can sing and rejoice and delight in God . . . you never enjoy the world.

THOMAS TRAHERNE (1637-1674)

I LIVE IN NOVA SCOTIA, ONE OF THREE MARITIME PROVINCES ON CANADA'S
Atlantic coast. I cannot help but think it is one of the most beautiful places
on God's earth. As the designation *Maritime* suggests, the history and

people of this place have been shaped by the sea. For much of the twentieth century "the Maritimes" were also one of Canada's economically struggling regions. Generations of young Maritimers have had to leave home and go "down the road" to larger urban centers in central Canada in search of work.

I remember a recent visit to Toronto. It was a brisk March day. My friend, a Maritimer who had lived in the city for years, had picked me up at the airport. On our way to his home we drove by the shores of Lake Ontario. I asked him, "Do the shores of the lake remind you of the ocean?" His response was immediate, full of feeling: "No, they only remind me how far away from the ocean I really am." I had anticipated such a response but had not expected it to be so passionate. You can take the man away from the ocean but you cannot take the ocean away from the man. My friend remains a Maritimer at heart.

Perhaps that sounds smug. Yes central Canadians may have the jobs and the money, but we have the ocean! But that is not the point. As any Maritimer knows, the ocean, truly appreciated and understood, fosters not pride but humility.

Meeting the Creator in Creation

Recently my brother-in-law participated in a church service at Terrance Bay on Nova Scotia's South Shore. The event commemorated the 123rd anniversary of the sinking of the SS *Atlantic*. (Over half of the 956 people on board perished in frigid Atlantic waters.) This year's service was notable in that some of the descendants of the only boy to survive, John Hindley, traveled north from the United States to take part. One young life was saved, and in that sense there is so much for which to be thankful. But the greater impression on participants was the sheer enormity of the loss, the host of descendants that could have been.

The ocean is no tame domesticated pet to be shown off to neighbors. I know that in part because I too have felt something of its fury. Seventeen years ago, on a cold December day, I was hit by a rogue wave at Peggy's Cove and battered into the fierce contours of granite in that beautiful but desolate place. I was lucky enough to escape with cuts and bruises, a badly sprained ankle and a ruined camera. I limped away, Jacob-like, with a new respect for the sheer power of the ocean.

Moving between fear of its power and delight in its beauty, I find my own place in those deep rhythms intrinsic to the ocean's life—the steady crash of surf as wave after wave curls in on itself, the bracing clarity of salt air breezes blowing onshore then offshore, the tides sallying back and forth, a global waltz orchestrated by the moon. These rhythms seduce and entrance. Nothing compares to that sober drunkenness, that heavy, exultantly weary fullness of body and spirit, that rapturous salt air mysticism every Maritimer feels at the end of a long day at the beach. Gratitude seems to be the only appropriate response.

Meister Eckhart, a medieval mystic, wrote that in the face of life's mysteries we need to accept that it is God, not us, who is at home in the universe.[1] At the edge of the ocean I realize that it is the ocean that is at home on this planet, not the land or those who dwell on it. Blue, not green, is the true native color of our world. All of us are sailors adrift on its ancient swell. G. K. Chesterton wrote that "the simplest truth about man is that he is a very strange being; almost in the sense of being a stranger on the earth."[2] At the edge of the ocean I am attuned to my strangeness. Standing on the edge of its vast expanse I somehow feel the smallness of my goodness, the goodness of my smallness.

Last summer my father told me about a spot on the shores of Prince Edward Island where my great-great-grandfather Edward Jorden, an immigrant from England, had chiseled words into the red sandstone cliffs of High Bank. Why would an ambitious pioneer farmer, with all the demanding duties of day-to-day life, take time to carve words into a cliff? Why would he spend hours writing a message into sandstone on a shore so obviously vulnerable to erosion? These questions were running through my mind as I descended the cliffs towards the shore. I found the etchings, perhaps eight feet above the waterline. Though a century's storms had worn it down, the message, miraculously, was still there—one simple word carved into red sandstone, "ETERNITY."

Celtic Christian Ecology

We live in a time when we are becoming acutely aware of the importance of our stance towards creation. Decades of uncompromising devotion to the gods of economic growth have left God's world battered and reeling.

In my own province the ocean's fish stocks have been decimated, threatening the very viability of coastal towns and villages that have lived off the largesse of the sea for centuries.

This economic crisis and the even more profound crisis at its heart—humanity's willful destruction of creation—led Nova Scotian composer of note Scott MacMillan and librettist Jennyfer Brickenden to write *The Celtic Mass for the Sea*. Texts for this work were drawn from ancient Celtic Christian sources. They speak with striking relevance to our contemporary crisis: "Preserve to our use the kindly fruits of the earth and restore and continue to us the blessings of the sea. Let not our faults or our frailty bring disaster upon us." Throughout *The Celtic Mass for the Sea* we hear the recurring refrain, "He who tramples on the world / He tramples on himself," words of deep ecological wisdom attributed to one of the greatest Celtic saints, Columba (521-597).

While others may look to quantum physics for a new understanding of the interconnectedness of life on this planet, or to an old paganism, hoping to revive a romantic vision of an enchanted world, I have found a hopeful place to start in Celtic Christian spirituality.

St. Patrick (c. 390-c. 461) was indeed a green saint. He signals the Celtic attitude to nature in one of his hymns:

> I bind unto myself today
> The strong name of the Trinity; . . .
> I bind unto myself today
> The virtues of the starlit heaven,
> The glorious sun's life-giving ray,
> The whiteness of the moon at even,
> The flashing of the lightning free,
> The whirling wind's tempestuous shocks,
> The stable earth, the deep salt sea,
> Around the old eternal rocks.[3]

Far from being aloof from the world, St. Patrick's God sustains and enlivens all. While the Celtic monasticism that St. Patrick inspired could be fiercely penitential and austere, it embodies a creation-embracing ecology. It celebrates a holy intimacy that connects all things human, natural and divine. "The Hermit's Song" captures something of the wondrous spirit of Celtic Christianity:

I wish, O Son of the living God, O ancient, eternal King,
For a hidden little hut in the wilderness that it may be my dwelling.

An all-grey little lake to be by its side.
A clear pool to wash away sins through the grace of the Holy Spirit.

Quite near, a beautiful wood around it on every side,
To nurse many-voiced birds, hiding it with its shelter. . . .

This is the husbandry I would take, I would choose, and will not hide
    it:
Fragrant leek, hens, speckled salmon, trout, bees.

Raiment and food enough for me from the King of fair fame,
And I to be sitting for a while praying God in every place.[4]

The Celtic saints celebrate creation as a kind of temple where God can
be met "in every place." While the setting of this "Song" is almost idyllic,
other Celtic monks chose to live in harsh places at the edge of the ocean.
These words have been attributed to St. Columba:

Delightful would it be to me to be . . .
On the pinnacle of a rock,
That I might often see
The face of the ocean;
That I might see its heaving waves
Over the wide ocean,
When they chant music to their Father
Upon the world's course;
That I might see its level of sparkling strand,
It would be no cause of sorrow;
That I might hear the roar by the side of the church
Of the surrounding sea;
That I might see its noble flocks
Over the watery ocean;
That I might see the sea-monsters,
The greatest of all wonders;
That I might see its ebb and flood
In their career . . .
That I might bless the Lord
Who conserves all,
Heaven with its countless bright orders,
Land, strand and flood.[5]

But one tale above all captures the genius of Celtic Christian ecology. St. Columba informed one of his brethren that in three days a stork would fall out of the sky onto the beach beside him. The bird would be near death, exhausted from a long flight. Columba instructed the man that he should take the bird to his home where he could feed it and attend to it. After three days Columba said, the bird would return with strength to its home across the ocean. The brother obeyed Columba, waited for the guest, took it home and nurtured it. After three days he watched the stork lift itself high into the sky on a straight course over the ocean.

The bird, three days sick then risen to new life, becomes a Christ figure. It is worth remembering that Jesus told his followers that in as much as they attended to the poor and blind and imprisoned they attended to him. In a bold exercise of Christian imagination St. Columba extends the principle to the whole created order, implying that Christ may be found in a thousand places.

Opening Our Eyes to Creation's Witness
Winters can be long and hard where I come from. The steady, biting cold and the extended hours of darkness can wear down one's spirits. By the time February comes I often find myself battling lethargy and discouragement. Winter holds the land, and my spirit, in its icy grip.

One February I was especially feeling the weight of the cold and dark. Going to work one morning I decided for some reason to forego my morning prayers and head out for a walk instead. Through the streets of our small town I trudged, out onto the dykelands, rich farmland built by Acadian settlers some three hundred years before. As I began to walk my eyes followed the lead of my spirit. They focused downward, watching my boots grudgingly crunch through hard-packed snow. Every step was labored.

Gradually, though, I lifted my head, and my eyes met a brilliant, shimmering, blue sky. My attention was riveted. Then across the dykelands, miles off in the distance, I saw the imposing red cliffs of Cape Blomidon. The grandeur of Blomidon led the aboriginal peoples of Nova Scotia, the Mi'kmaq, to declare it the resting place of their god, Glooscap. My cold dull spirits were jolted by the sheer beauty of what I was seeing. I walked with new energy, then I stopped and slowly turned my body around again and again to take in the full splendor of that scene. "Open your eyes," I heard from somewhere. I continued my walk with those three words ringing in my heart. It was as if I had woken up and found myself in a new world. My spirits were irretrievably lifted well beyond the reach of winter doldrums. In days that followed I continued to hear the healing echo of those words: "Open your eyes." I was given new eyes, not only to see the beauty of creation but also to see God's work in so many other areas of my life.

The Celtic saints challenge us to develop disciplines that help us pay more attention to creation. Even in urban settings we can regularly give thanks to God for his creation gifts if we have the eyes to see them—warm winds, bright sunshine, trees that line streets, public parks and gardens, even the bright swash of color that greets us in the produce section of our supermarket. At every meal we eat of the fruits of creation. With eyes open we will cultivate a spirit of gratitude. We will be drawn to God and to a fresh accounting of his mercies in the daily gifts of creation.

The Celtic saints met God in the wonder of his world. Their delight in nature shows little restraint, except in one matter. They insist that creation itself should never be the focus of worship. Creation and Creator are distinct. Only God is deserving of worship. But far from distracting them, creation's gifts drew Celtic saints into communion with God. Here is the witness of another Celtic monk:

> For I inhabit a wood
> unknown but to my God
> my house of hazel and ash
> as an old hut in a rath . . .
> For music I
> have pines, my tall
> music-pines
> So who can I
> envy here, my
> gentle Christ?[6]

My friend Bruce is a contemporary believer who loves to be close to nature. While he lives in a suburban neighborhood and feels the time pressures of every entrepreneur, for the past few years he has made a point of starting each day with a walk to nearby parks. There in those small havens of nature he drinks up the beauty of creation and prays. Growing up he was taught to be suspicious of any intense love of creation because it indicated a lack of balance in one's theology, even a lack of devotion to Christ. Bruce's experience in adulthood suggests the opposite. Like the Celtic saints Bruce feels closest to God in watching the daily growth of wildflowers at the edge of a pond. There prayers to his gentle Christ flow most freely.

Caring for Creation as a Spiritual Discipline

I have found the Celtic saints' love of creation to be joyously contagious. They may help us rekindle our delight in nature and its Creator. But the opening chapters of Genesis make it clear that while we should find joy in creation—mirroring God's delight—we are also set in this garden to care for it. Few would argue, as we enter a new millennium, that one of humanity's most important challenges is to relearn, and to relearn quickly, what it means to have a profound sense of responsibility for creation. Literally everything is at stake. No one should feel the weight of responsibility more than Christians. Environmental stewardship is part of following Jesus: "All things have been created through him and for him" (Col 1:16). Decisions to use our cars less, to avoid plastic containers, to set up a composter in our backyard are not only wise, creation-sensitive choices. They are also habits of the heart that honor the beauty of God's trust to us, opportunities to mirror his own sustaining love and care for all he has created. Approached in the right way they become spiritual disciplines that grow out of humility, a rightful sense of our place in the order of creation. They flow from a charitable heart that burns with God's love for the whole creation.

Celtic Christians lived out a green faith. While given to extreme asceticism, they were profoundly earthy. The body was disciplined but affirmed and celebrated. In striving for the eternal they found rapture in the temporal beauty of creation. In hungering for relationship with the God above creation they discovered a vital sense of his presence in creation. They were robustly orthodox (St. Patrick "made them pass from the cult of the sun to that of the 'true son who is Christ' "[7]), but they were still able to appropriate what was healthy in the vibrant pagan culture around them, including its deep sense of connectedness to nature. Celtic Christians did not live in an enchanted world where nature was simply and idolatrously identified with God but in a world charged with the grandeur of God, a world deserving only the deepest wonder and care.

Questions for Reflection and Discussion

1. What strikes you about the example of the Celtic saints and their relationship to creation?

2. What experiences have you had of meeting the Creator in creation?

3. What might you do that would help you meet God in creation on a more regular basis?

4. What are some of the daily gifts of creation that you easily overlook?

5. What practical initiatives do you take or could you take to exercise care for God's creation?

6. In what sense might they be spiritual disciplines?

APPENDIX

READING THE SAINTS

C. S. LEWIS ACCUSED MODERN PERSONS OF "CHRONOLOGICAL SNOBBERY"—THE CONVICTION that whatever is newer must be better than what is older. Unfortunately, "chronological snobbery" afflicts the devotional reading of many Christians. As a sad consequence, the soul-building power of the devotional classics lies untapped.

It is important to note that reading the spiritual masters calls for a different sort of reading than many of us normally practice. Most of the time when we read, we read for information. In reading devotionally we read not for information but for transformation. Our goal is not to plug more information into our minds. Instead we seek to penetrate spiritual truths that will transform us from the very core of our being.

For practical tips on the art of spiritual reading I could hardly do better than to summarize the five points John Wesley makes in his "Advice on Spiritual Reading" (1735).

1. Set aside time on a regular basis for spiritual reading. It does not need to be a long time. Consistency is the key.

2. Prepare yourself for reading. Quiet your heart. Approach God in prayer. Ask that he would help you see the truth, and have the courage to follow through on its implications for your living.

3. Read slowly, seriously and attentively. Take time to pause in your reading. Focus intently on the truth of a passage. Allow it to sink into your heart. Open your heart to the enlightenment of God's grace.

4. Intersperse your reading with short prayers to God. Make note of helpful sayings or sage pieces of advice. Memorize them or write them down. You may want to share them with a friend.

5. Conclude your reading with a short prayer to God. Ask that seeds sown in your heart would bring forth a rich harvest of obedience and devotion.

In summation, remember that spiritual reading is pointless if it is filling our heads without stirring our hearts.

For further reading of the saints explored in this book, I would make the following suggestions. (I make no pretense of being a scholar with comprehensive knowledge of all the relevant material. I will merely point you in directions that have turned out to be helpful for me).

John Bunyan

The Pilgrim's Progress was as wildly popular in Catholic Spain as it was in Protestant England. Its message is universal. After *The Pilgrim's Progress*, Bunyan's autobiographical *Grace Abounding to the Chief of Sinners* is recommended. Other Puritan classics include Richard Baxter's *The Saints' Everlasting Rest* and Jonathan Edwards's *Religious Affections*.

Julian of Norwich

Though she is widely regarded as a major mystic figure in the history of the church, Thomas Merton reminded us that she was a penetrating theologian as well. Her *Showings* (sometimes titled *Revelations,* or *Revelations of Divine Love*) is all we have from the pen of this remarkable woman. In this work she recounts and meditates on sixteen visions she experienced.

John of Ruysbroeck

Ruysbroeck was Evelyn Underhill's favorite mystical writer. *The Adornment of the Spiritual Marriage* (sometimes titled *The Spiritual Espousals*) is his classic work. *The Sparkling Stone* and *The Book of Supreme Truth* are other major works. Ruysbroeck is not always easy to read, but he rewards those willing to study and digest his work.

Bernard of Clairvaux

On many counts Bernard is a giant of the faith. It would be hard to conceive of a mind and heart more saturated with knowledge of the Scriptures and burning devotion to Jesus. His two short works *On Conversion* and *On Loving God* are compelling introductions to his spirit and thought.

John Newton

The subtitle of his *Collected Letters* (sometimes titled *Cardiphonia*) is a mouthful, but it is also telling: *The Utterance of the Heart in the Course of a Real Correspondence*. His letters were bestsellers in their own day, and it is easy to see why. Newton's hymns, as well as those of his gifted contemporaries, Charles Wesley, Isaac Watts and William Cowper, also make for a feast of spiritual reading.

Origen
One of the great church fathers, Origen was equal part theologian and man of prayer. For him, in fact, the two tasks were one. In addition to its practical guidance on the preliminaries of prayer, *On Prayer* contains Origen's influential exposition of the Lord's Prayer.

The Desert Fathers
On one level the sayings of the desert fathers are delightfully quirky and engaging. On another they are frighteningly perceptive and probing. Either way, they are not easily forgotten. Collections of their sayings are available. Henri Nouwen's *The Way of the Heart* is a helpful introduction to the spirituality of the desert and its relevance for our day.

Evelyn Underhill
Modern-day mystic, scholar, spiritual director and retreat leader Evelyn Underhill has left an enduring mark on twentieth-century spirituality. After her *Letters* I would recommend reading a spiritual classic from the pen of her mentor, *Letters from Baron Friedrich von Hügel to a Niece*.

Aelred of Rievaulx
The epitaph on Aelred's tomb reads, "No sooner have you read him than you want to read him again." *On Spiritual Friendship* and *The Mirror of Charity* are his two principal works. For a learned and fascinating overview of the Cistercian tradition (Bernard and Aelred are key figures), read Jean Leclercq's *The Love of Learning and the Desire for God*.

Margery Kempe
The Book of Margery Kempe is our sole window into the life of Margery—but what a window and what a life. Other classics of English spirituality in the fourteenth century include Richard Rolle's *The Fire of Love* and Walter Hilton's *The Ladder of Perfection*.

George Herbert
Simone Weil, the great French thinker of the twentieth century, was converted on reading Herbert's poem "Love III." As she read, "Christ came down and took

possession of me." Weil's response is a dramatic example of what many have experienced—George Herbert's poems, collected in *The Temple*, make for powerful spiritual reading. For another sample of Anglican spirituality read the beautiful prayers of one of Herbert's schoolmasters, Lancelot Andrewes, collected in his *Private Devotions.*

The Celtic Saints

Celtic spirituality is all the rage these days. Unfortunately, much of the interest is focused on pagan Celtic spirituality. An introduction to the world of the Celtic saints needs a wise guide. Esther de Waal is the most knowledgeable and discerning guide I have found. *The Celtic Way of Prayer* and *Every Earthly Blessing: Celebrating a Spirituality of Creation* are two of her works; both are full of generous quotations from the saints themselves.

Further Reading

Two enduring classics of devotional reading are not on this list but deserve special mention: Augustine's *Confessions* and Thomas à Kempis's *The Imitation of Christ.* Both warrant a lifetime of reading and rereading. For a sampling of many of the spiritual masters, I highly recommend Richard Foster's *Devotional Classics.*

Notes

Chapter 1/Journeying on the Road
[1]John Bunyan, *The Pilgrim's Progress,* ed. Roger Sharrock (London: Penguin, 1965), p. 77.
[2]Ibid., p. 114.
[3]Ibid., p. 121.
[4]Ibid., p. 107.
[5]Ibid., p. 156.
[6]Ibid., p. 161.
[7]Ibid., p. 207.
[8]Ibid., pp. 170, 173.

Chapter 2/Turning Our Eyes on Jesus
[1]Julian of Norwich, *Showings,* trans. Edmund Colledge and James Walsh (Toronto: Paulist, 1978), p. 319.
[2]Ibid., p. 246.
[3]Ibid., p. 319.
[4]Peter Kreeft, *Heaven: The Heart's Deepest Longing* (San Francisco: Harper & Row, 1980), p. 61.
[5]Charles Williams, *The Descent of the Dove* (London: Faber & Faber, 1950), p. 131.

Chapter 3/Practicing the Presence of Jesus
[1]John of Ruysbroeck, *The Adornment of the Spiritual Marriage; The Sparkling Stone; The Book of Supreme Truth,* trans. C. A. Wynschenk (London: J. M. Dent, 1916), p. 10. All citations here are from *The Adornment of the Spiritual Marriage.*
[2]Ibid.
[3]Ibid., p. 17.
[4]Annie Dillard, *Pilgrim at Tinker Creek* (New York: Harper Magazine Press, 1974), p. 33.
[5]John of Ruysbroeck, *Adornment,* p. 5.
[6]Ibid., p. 17.
[7]*The Way of a Pilgrim,* trans. R. M. French (San Francisco: Harper & Row, 1952), p. 17.
[8]John of Ruysbroeck, *Adornment,* p. 18.
[9]Ibid.
[10]Ibid.
[11]W. H. Auden, "For the Time Being: A Christmas Oratorio," in *Collected Poems* (New York: Random House, 1976), p. 274.
[12]John of Ruysbroeck, *Adornment,* p. 48.
[13]Ibid., p. 4.
[14]Ibid., p. 11.

Chapter 4/Reaching the Highest Love
[1]Blaise Pascal, *Pensées,* trans. A. J. Krailsheimer (London: Penguin, 1966), p. 64.

[2]*The Works of Rev. John Newton* (London: J. Adlard, 1816), 6:98.

[3]In this discussion I am particularly indebted to Gerald May, *Care of Mind/Care of Spirit* (New York: HarperCollins, 1992), pp. 66-73, and Henri Nouwen, *The Return of the Prodigal Son* (New York: Doubleday, 1992), pp. 98-109.

[4]John Donne, *Devotions upon Emergent Occasions* (Ann Arbor: University of Michigan Press, 1959), p. 41, prayer 6.

[5]Jonathan Edwards, *The Religious Affections* (Edinburgh: Banner of Truth, 1961), pp. 168-69.

[6]Bernard of Clairvaux, "On Loving God," in *Selected Works*, trans. G. R. Evans (New York: Paulist, 1987), p. 194.

[7]Pascal, *Pensées*, pp. 64-65.

[8]Bernard, "On Loving God," p. 186.

[9]Ibid., p. 204.

Chapter 5/Working Through Spiritual Dryness

[1]*The Works of Rev. John Newton* (London: J. Adlard, 1816), 6:64.

[2]Ibid., p. 65.

Chapter 6/Combating Prayerlessness

[1]Origen, "On Prayer," in *Origen: An Exhortation to Martyrdom, Prayer and Selected Works*, trans. Rowan A. Greer (New York: Paulist, 1979), p. 86.

[2]Ibid., p. 164.

[3]Ibid., p. 99.

[4]Ibid., p. 98.

[5]*The Life of Saint Teresa of Ávila by Herself*, trans. J. M. Cohen (London: Penguin, 1957), p. 37.

[6]Cited by Timothy Ware, *The Orthodox Church* (London: Penguin, 1993), p. 67.

[7]Origen, "On Prayer," pp. 164-65.

[8]Ibid., p. 166.

[9]Ibid., p. 167.

Chapter 7/Resisting Temptation

[1]Thomas à Kempis, *The Imitation of Christ*, trans. Ronald Knox and Michael Oakley (London: Burns & Oates, 1959), p. 113.

[2]Thomas Merton, ed., *The Wisdom of the Desert* (New York: New Directions, 1960), pp. 56-57.

[3]Ibid., p. 34.

[4]Ibid., p. 43.

[5]Taken from lecture notes. Here, as in so much of this book, I am greatly indebted to the inspirational teaching of Dr. James Houston.

[6]Merton, *Wisdom of the Desert*, p. 48.

[7]Cited in Benedicta Ward, ed., *The Sayings of the Desert Fathers* (London: Mowbray, 1981), p. 9.

[8]Merton, *Wisdom of the Desert*, p. 72.

[9]Thomas Merton, *Contemplative Prayer* (New York: Doubleday, 1990), p. 22.

[10]Merton, *Wisdom of the Desert*, p. 50.

[11]Richard Rolle, *The Fire of Love,* trans. Clifton Wolters (Middlesex, U.K.: Penguin, 1972), p. 113.

[12]St. Augustine, cited in *Classic Love: Timeless Wisdom from Classic Writers,* ed. Robert Backhouse (London: Hodder & Stoughton, 1995), p. 102.

Chapter 8/Overcoming Discouragement

[1]Evelyn Underhill, "Preface to the Twelfth Edition," in *Mysticism: The Preeminent Study in the Nature and Development of Spiritual Consciousness* (New York: Doubleday, 1990), p. xiv.

[2]*The Letters of Evelyn Underhill,* ed. Charles Williams (London: Longmans, Green, 1943), pp. 126-27.

[3]Ibid., p. 183.

[4]Ibid., p. 252.

[5]Ibid., p. 316.

[6]Ibid., p. 243.

[7]Ibid., p. 96.

[8]John of the Cross, "The Dark Night," in *Selected Writings,* trans. Kieran Kavanaugh (New York: Paulist, 1987), p. 173.

[9]*Letters of Evelyn Underhill,* p. 96.

[10]Jonathan Edwards, *The Religious Affections* (Edinburgh: Banner of Truth, 1961), p. 89.

[11]*Letters of Evelyn Underhill,* p. 169.

[12]Ibid., p. 315.

[13]Ibid., p. 272.

[14]Ibid., pp. 262-63.

[15]Søren Kierkegaard's *Journals and Papers,* trans. Howard V. Hong and Edna H. Hong (Bloomington: Indiana University Press, 1970), 2:99.

[16]This phrase from Baron von Hügel has stayed with me since I first read it. Unfortunately I have been unable to locate its precise location in his classic work *Letters from Baron Friedrich von Hügel to a Niece,* ed. Gwendolen Greene (Chicago: Henry Regnery, 1955).

[17]Cited by Martin Thorton, *English Spirituality* (Cambridge, Mass.: Cowley, 1986), p. 215.

[18]*Letters of Evelyn Underhill,* p. 306.

[19]Ibid., p. 312.

[20]Ibid., p. 311.

Chapter 9/Celebrating Spiritual Friendships

[1]Aelred of Rievaulx, *On Spiritual Friendship,* trans. Mary Eugenia Laker (Washington, D.C.: Cistercian, 1974), p. 45.

[2]Cited by Louis Bouyer, *The Cistercian Heritage,* trans. Elizabeth A. Livingstone (London: A. R. Mowbray, 1958), pp. 138-39.

[3]Aelred of Rievaulx, *Treatises/Pastoral Prayer,* trans. R. Penelope Lawson (Kalamazoo, Mich.: Cistercian, 1971), pp. 114-15.

[4]Walter Daniel, *Life of Aelred,* ed. F. M. Powicke (London: Nelson, 1950), p. 40.

[5]Aelred, *On Spiritual Friendship,* p. 51.

[6]Ibid., p. 53.

[7]Ibid., p. 62.

[8]Ibid., pp. 65-66.

[9]Ibid., p. 72.
[10]Ibid., p. 58.
[11]Ibid., p. 72.
[12]Ibid., p. 68
[13]Cited by M. Basil Pennington in Aelred, *Spiritual Friendship,* p. 115.
[14]Aelred, *Spiritual Friendship,* p. 122.

Chapter 10/Loving the Unlovable
[1]*The Book of Margery Kempe,* trans. W. Butler-Bowdon (New York: Devin-Adair, 1944), pp. 41-42.
[2]Martin Thorton, *English Spirituality* (Cambridge, Mass.: Cowley, 1986), pp. 222-24, 297.
[3]Charles Williams, *The Descent of the Dove* (London: Faber & Faber, 1950), p. 144.
[4]George Eliot, *Silas Marner* (Toronto: Thomas Nelson, n.d.), p. 159.

Chapter 11/Inspiring Others to Godliness
[1]Izaak Walton, *The Lives of John Donne and George Herbert,* Harvard Classics 15, ed. Charles W. Eliot (New York: P. F. Collier, 1909), p. 376.
[2]Cited in ibid., p. 395.
[3]Ibid., p. 397.
[4]Cited in ibid., p. 405.
[5]Cited in ibid., p. 407.
[6]Cited in ibid., p. 417.
[7]Nicholas Ferrar, "The Dedication to *The Temple*," in George Herbert, *The Country Parson and The Temple,* ed. John N. Wall Jr. (New York: Paulist, 1981), p. 119.
[8]Cited by Amy M. Charles, *A Life of George Herbert* (Ithaca. N.Y.: Cornell University Press, 1977), p. 176.
[9]Herbert, *Country Parson,* p. 68.
[10]Ibid., p. 57.
[11]Ibid., p. 90.
[12]Ibid., p. 95.
[13]Ibid., p. 109.
[14]Cited in Walton, *Lives of John Donne and George Herbert,* p. 414.

Chapter 12/Caring for Creation
[1]Cited by Annie Dillard, *Holy the Firm* (New York: Harper & Row, 1977), p. 62.
[2]G. K. Chesterton, *The Everlasting Man* (New York: Dodd, Mead, 1925), p. 19.
[3]Cited in *Earthkeeping in the Nineties,* ed. Loren Wilkinson (Grand Rapids, Mich.: Eerdmans, 1991), p. 139.
[4]Cited in *Celtic Christianity: Ecology and Holiness,* ed. William Parker Marsh and Christopher Bamford (West Stockbridge, Mass.: Lindisfarne, 1987), pp. 70-71.
[5]Cited in *Celtic Christianity,* pp. 114-15.
[6]Cited by Pierre Riche, "Spirituality in Celtic and Germanic Society," in *Christian Spirituality: Origins to the Twelfth Century,* ed. Bernard McGinn, John Meyendorff and Jean Leclercq (New York: Crossroad, 1985), pp. 170-71.
[7]Ibid., p. 166.